SECOND EDITION

MEDIATED
Learning

This manual is dedicated to Professor Reuven Feuerstein, whose belief system, theory of cognition and cognitive modifiability, insight into cognitive dysfunction, and parameters of Mediated Learning Experience constitute the inspiration and mainspring for our work. We are thankful for his continued support of our efforts in the interpretation and applications of his ideas and concepts in this publication.

SECOND EDITION

MEDIATED

Learning

Teaching, Tasks,

and Tools to Unlock

Cognitive Potential

Second Edition of
Mediated Learning In and Out of the Classroom

Mandia Mentis

Marilyn Dunn-Bernstein

Martene Mentis

Foreword by
Reuven Feuerstein

CORWIN PRESS
A SAGE Publications Company
Thousand Oaks, CA 91320

Illustrations by Martene Mentis.

For information:

Corwin Press
A Sage Publications Company
2455 Teller Road
Thousand Oaks, California 91320
www.corwinpress.com

Sage Publications Ltd.
1 Oliver's Yard
55 City Road
London EC1Y 1SP
United Kingdom

Sage Publications India Pvt. Ltd.
B 1/I 1 Mohan Cooperative Industrial Area
Mathura Road, New Delhi 110 044
India

Sage Publications Asia-Pacific Pte. Ltd.
33 Pekin Street #02-01
Far East Square
Singapore 048763

Printed in the United States of America

Library of Congress Cataloging-in-Publication Data

Mentis, M.
Mediated learning: Teaching, tasks, and tools to unlock cognitive potential/Mandia Mentis, Marilyn Dunn-Bernstein, and Martene Mentis.—2nd ed.
    p. cm.
Includes bibliographical references and index.
ISBN 978-1-4129-5069-5 (cloth)
ISBN 978-1-4129-5070-1 (pbk.)
    1. Thought and thinking—Study and teaching. 2. Cognition in children. 3. Learning, Psychology of. I. Dunn-Bernstein, Marilyn J., 1952—II. Mentis, Martene. III. Title.

LB1590.3.M46 2007
370.15'2—dc22   2006102699

This book is printed on acid-free paper.

12 13 14 15 11 10 9 8 7 6 5 4 3

Acquisitions Editor:	Cathy Hernandez
Editorial Assistant:	Megan Bedell
Production Editor:	Melanie Birdsall
Copy Editor:	Gretchen Treadwell
Typesetter:	C&M Digitals (P) Ltd.
Proofreader:	Dennis W. Webb
Indexer:	Naomi Linzer
Cover Designer:	Karine Hovsepian

Contents

Foreword

The theory of Mediated Learning Experience (MLE) dates back to the 1950s. I developed it to explain individuals' different propensities for learning. For example, young adults emigrating from different cultures to Israel have shown different levels of learning propensity in adapting to Israel's technology-oriented society. Some of these differences are explained by the nature of the cultures from which these individuals came. What is more interesting, however, are the differences in the learning propensities among individuals belonging to the same culture. In this respect, the observed intragroup differences were often greater than the intergroup ones.

Low-functioning individuals among the culturally different groups were able to adapt to the new culture's stimuli and requirements by direct exposure. Other individuals, whom we later defined as "culturally deprived," were able to benefit not at all or only very little from their exposure to the new culture. They were able to integrate only marginally.

Similar observations have been made by researchers attempting to define the cognitive structure of culturally different groups. The researchers found that there were differences that could not be explained by the culture the immigrants came from. Thus, they dispelled the all too often emitted hypothesis that certain cultures "deprive" their members. As a result, we linked the differences in learning propensity to an individuals' exposure through MLE to their own particular culture, irrespective of its nature or level of conceptualization, technology, or institutionalized education.

Culturally different individuals have become "different" by learning their own culture. This learning experience, usually gained through an MLE process, turns individuals into efficient learners. They use their previously acquired learning experiences to confront a new culture. Culturally deprived individuals, on the other hand, have not been exposed to their own culture. They have not learned to learn. Therefore, it is difficult for them to adapt to the new, more complex conditions of life, which require them to use a learning process for which they have not developed the necessary cognitive tools.

Cultural deprivation, in contradistinction to cultural difference, is a universal phenomenon. It can be observed in a large variety of ethnic, socioeconomical, and professional environments. Cultural deprivation and lack of MLE may be determined by (1) exogenous factors, such as cultural environmental conditions, where parents and/or peer groups do not offer mediation or cultural transmission; or (2) mediation that does not penetrate the mental system due to internal physiological conditions. Cultural deprivation (i.e., lack of MLE), irrespective of its etiology, exogenous or endogenous, lowers individuals' flexibility and plasticity. This makes it difficult for them to adapt to new conditions of life through a learning process.

Culturally deprived individuals need a special form and level of intensity of MLE in order to overcome these difficulties.

Twenty or more years after its inception, the theory and practice of MLE have become the focus of intensive research. Its meaning extends over large areas of interest in the human condition. Several hundred papers have looked into the relationships MLE has had with other theoretical positions in philosophy, neuropsychology, and cognitive science. These papers addressed not only the possibility of using MLE as a theory to explain the ontology of human cognitive development, but also the possibility of turning the operationalized concepts implied by MLE into guidelines for an applied system. This system would allow individuals to be more adaptable and modifiable, thereby allowing them to confront today's cultural requirements.

Work has also been done by Camusso, Cardinet, Haywood, Lidz, Klein, S. Feuerstein, Rafi Feuerstein, Burges, and Paravy that focuses on MLE's parameters and their relationships to various areas of human development.

In addition, I have contributed to the pioneering work of Yael Mintsker, Nilli Ben Shachar, and others in translating the theory of MLE into operational modalities of interaction between parents and children, caregivers and children, and teachers and students. The Learning Potential Assessment Device (LPAD) manuals include part of this work, as MLE plays a pivotal role in the LPAD. The LPAD includes samples of change in the cognitive structure of an individual. They are interpreted and used as a basis for a profile of the individual's modifiability.

The teacher's guides for the Instrumental Enrichment (IE) program also use MLE as the main modality to shape the interaction of "teacher-materials-exercises-students." The parameters of MLE are used in a focused way in the execution of the IE program.

Mediated Learning: Teaching, Tasks, and Tools to Unlock Cognitive Potential is a continuation of the effort to operationalize the theory of MLE, Structural Cognitive Modifiability, Cognitive Dysfunction, and the Cognitive Map. The great value of this book is that it is presented to the reader as a wonderful paradigm of MLE and the various parameters. A valuable addenda to previous works, it serves educators, parents, and counselors who are applying the LPAD or IE. It is also useful for those in community counseling situations. In general, it is an asset for those trying to find new ways of reaching out to the many people who need a real change in their interaction with their children, students, or peers.

I am gratified by the publication of this book, written by a group of people who have shown their deep understanding and true devotion to the quality of life that can be produced through mediated learning and metacognition.

—*Professor Reuven Feuerstein*
Founder and Head of International Center for the
Enhancement of Learning Potential and
the Hadassah-Wizo-Canada Research Institute

Preface

The notion that education should develop the cognitive abilities of students, that is, that students should be taught how to think, has been treated in a variety of ways by those involved in education. At one extreme, it has been a notion more honored in its breach than in its observance. In fact, many satirists have portrayed traditional schooling as an antidote to thinking, and thinking as a danger to institutionalized education.

In many countries, the dominant educational ideologies have recognized that to teach children to think would be incompatible with the maintenance of the status quo. In those situations, education does not create thinking students and autonomous learners.

Only relatively recently (in the past few decades) have practical tools become available that translate the rather pious resolution of "we must teach children how to think" into a practicable activity. Indeed, numerous thinking skills programs have resulted from the increasing emphasis that cognitive psychology has placed on the educability of intelligence. Feuerstein's theories of Mediated Learning Experience (MLE) and Structural Cognitive Modifiability have been essential in these developments.

This book aims to extend the practical application of various dimensions of Feuerstein's theory and belief system, especially in relation to Mediated Learning Experience, Deficient Cognitive Functions, and the Cognitive Map. The first edition of this book, *Mediated Learning In and Out of the Classroom*, arose out of the work of the Cognitive Research Program, which was established within the Division of Specialized Education at the University of Witwatersrand, South Africa, in 1990. The work is based on extensive research and implementation and adaptation of Feuerstein's Instrumental Enrichment Program of Thinking Skills in a variety of educational settings internationally. Feuerstein's theory and techniques have served as the cornerstone of and springboard for this publication. We are greatly indebted to him and to his team for their vision, their inspiration, and their training.

WHAT IS MEDIATED LEARNING?

"Because of . . ." statements are not uncommon to hear in the staffrooms and classrooms of most schools. These statements convey the same general message, although the specific details differ: "Because of his low IQ, he should be given a simplified curriculum"; "Because she is hearing-impaired, she will not be able to take rigorous academic courses"; "Because of her poor academic test scores, she should not plan to study beyond high school"; "Because of the alcohol abuse in the home, he will struggle in class."

The response to these "Because of . . ." statements is contained in the educational theory and research on which this book is based. This response is that education will improve only when educators realize that rather than perpetuate the misguided emphasis on the predictive value of tests scores or genetic factors or environmental conditions, the school's task is, irrespective of these factors, to develop the student's underlying cognitive functions (i.e., the ability to learn and become an autonomous thinker) and intrinsic motivation (i.e., love of learning and extension of interests).

Rather than pessimistically predict future outcomes based on the student's current low level of functioning, the teacher should optimistically view this as the baseline for potential change in the student's ability to learn. This change should be seen as being dependent on the quality of teacher-student and parent-student interaction. It is through this interaction that the cognitive and motivational functions needed for learning will be modified. This approach is based on having a belief that change is possible, and then having the skills and strategies to bring about that change.

Our response to the "Because of. . . ." statements about IQ scores or genetic factors or environmental concerns is to change the "Because" to "Despite" and thereby change the focus from doing less to doing more. Rewording these statements would change our thinking from blaming the learner to empowering the teacher. A far more optimistic statement would be "Despite a low IQ or hearing impairment or autism or alcoholism, the right kind of mediated learning can offer the potential for cognitive change to achieve independence and autonomy." This approach would be in keeping with the theory and practice of Reuven Feuerstein—it is this theory of cognitive modifiability and mediated learning that will be explored in this book.

WHO IS REUVEN FEUERSTEIN?

Reuven Feuerstein is an internationally renowned Israeli professor of psychology who has been working in the field of child development for over 50 years. Through his work with low-functioning and disadvantaged individuals, he developed innovative methods of testing and teaching that have been applied worldwide. Along with other contemporary psychologists, he rejects the static belief that individuals are born with a certain intelligence that remains fixed throughout life. In contrast, he has shown that individuals have the potential to change and are modifiable if provided with the opportunities to engage in the right kind of interaction. This "potential to change" is described by Feuerstein as Structural Cognitive Modifiability, and the "right kind of interaction" as Mediated Learning Experience. Through mediated learning, learners can change the way they think (cognitive modifiability) and develop the efficient thinking skills that are necessary to become an autonomous and independent learner. In addition, Feuerstein has constructed a list of Cognitive Functions that are the prerequisites or building blocks of efficient thinking. These building blocks of efficient thinking can be taught by adapting the teaching task using a Cognitive Map. Together, Structural Cognitive Modifiability (as the belief in change), Mediated Learning Experience (as the method of change), and the Cognitive Functions and Cognitive Map (as the tools of change) can pave the way to effective learning.

WHAT IS THIS BOOK ALL ABOUT?

This book covers the principles and application of Feuerstein's theories of Structural Cognitive Modifiability (SCM), Mediated Learning Experience (MLE), the Cognitive Functions, and the Cognitive Map.

Part I. Metalearning: Structural Cognitive Modifiability

This part explains Feuerstein's theory of modifiability and belief in change. It outlines the difference between passively accepting a learner's low level of functioning (passive acceptance) and attempting to actively modify and bring about change in learning (active modification). This part invites reflection on a case study used to illustrate the different belief systems in learning and teaching. This part on SCM is headed Metalearning, as it focuses our thinking on learning.

Part II. Metateaching: Mediated Learning Experience

This part explains Feuerstein's theory of interaction, Mediated Learning Experience, and how using MLE can bring about changes in cognition. Feuerstein has 12 key criteria of MLE and each one of these provides a different approach of interacting with the learner. Examples and ideas for using MLE in teaching, parenting, and counseling are provided. This part on MLE is headed Metateaching, as it focuses our thinking on teaching.

Part III. Metacognition: Cognitive Functions and Dysfunctions

This part explains Feuerstein's list of thinking skills—the cognitive functions. It shows the relationship between the input, elaboration, and output phases of thinking and demonstrates how a teacher might identify a student who is experiencing cognitive difficulties in the classroom. Strategies are provided for the teacher to overcome cognitive difficulties that are linked to the criteria of mediation. This part on Cognitive Functions and Dysfunctions is headed Metacognition, as it focuses our thinking on thinking.

Part IV. Metatask: The Cognitive Map

This part explains Feuerstein's tool to analyze a task. It shows how a teacher might vary or change a learning task or experience to identify how and where a learner is experiencing cognitive difficulties. Examples are provided of how the Cognitive Map can be used as a tool for analyzing and manipulating a teaching experience to identify cognitive dysfunctions and improve thinking. This part on the Cognitive Map is headed Metatask, as it focuses our thinking on the teaching and learning task.

The ideas and applications presented in this book can be used by anyone concerned with the learning potential of students—educators, community workers, school counselors, psychologists, parents, and caregivers—to

- Encourage autonomous learning
- Unlock a student's potential
- Promote the use of effective thinking skills
- Develop a positive belief in the propensity to change
- Improve parenting
- Remediate cognitive dysfunctions
- Analyze a student's cognitive strengths and weaknesses
- Modify a teaching task to promote learning

HOW TO USE THIS BOOK

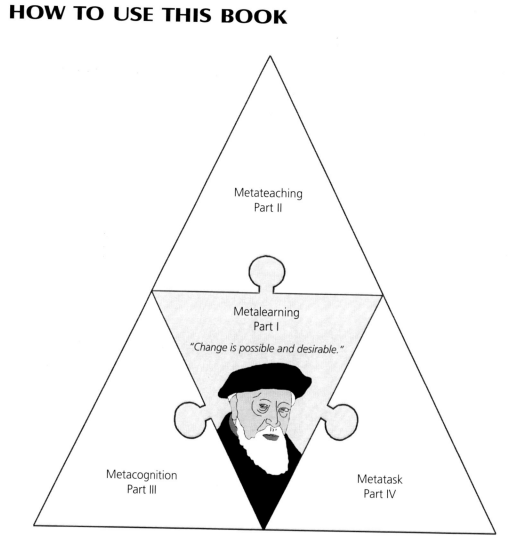

As indicated in the diagram, Feuerstein's theory and approach is represented in this book as consisting of a central core theory in the middle of the triangle and three operational techniques at the three corners of the triangle. Each of these points of the triangle focuses on the triad of the learning process: the learner, the teacher, and the task.

This can be illustrated as follows:

- At the core of the triangle is Feuerstein's theory of Structural Cognitive Modifiability—the belief that all individuals have the potential to change and learn.

This is the subject of Part I: Metalearning and poses the following question for reflection:

- What do you believe about learning—do you passively accept the status quo or attempt to actively modify and bring about cognitive change in the learner?

At the first point of the triangle, the focus is on the teacher/parent/caregiver—and the tool or technique is the "right kind of interaction" called the Mediated Learning Experience. This is the subject of Part II: Metateaching and poses the following question for educators:

- What kind of interaction or mediation is needed to bring about cognitive change in the learner?

At the second point of the triangle, the focus is on the learner—and the technique offered is a checklist of thinking skills—the Cognitive Functions and Dysfunctions. This is the subject of Part III: Metacognition and poses the following question:

- What cognitive dysfunctions are evident and how can the educator change these and develop efficient thinking skills?

At the third point of the triangle, the focus is on the task—and the technique offered is a map to analyze the teaching experience—the Cognitive Map. This is the subject of Part IV: Metatask and poses the following question:

- How can the learning task be analyzed to identify and develop efficient thinking skills?

The triangle helps to illustrate how the four concepts of Feuerstein's approach are linked. At the heart of the triangle is the theory or belief in modifiability. Once an educator believes that change is possible, the skills or techniques to bring about change are needed, and the three corners of the triangle are these techniques: for the teacher—Mediated Learning; for the learner—the Cognitive Functions; and for the task—the Cognitive Map.

It is the questions relating to these four elements of Feuerstein's theory and practice that will be answered throughout this book.

Acknowledgments

The first edition of this book, *Mediated Learning In and Out of the Classroom*, was a product of the Cognitive Research Programme team of the University of the Witwatersrand. The authors would like to acknowledge and thank two significant members of our original writing team for their contributions to the first edition, Mervyn Skuy and Fleur Durbach, University of the Witwatersrand, South Africa.

This second edition of the book has drawn on the current authors' continued work in applying Feuerstein's approaches through research projects, training workshops, and teaching in various educational contexts. This has taken us into classrooms, lecture rooms, and homes in South Africa, Israel, Australia, New Zealand and the United States working with students with diverse learning needs. We are indebted to these learners for the insights that they continually provide. The authors would also like to thank all those who have contributed through their participation in the training workshops of the Cognitive Research Programme and the Australasian Institute for Learning Enhancement. We acknowledge the voice of the practitioners, therapists, teachers, and parents who we have worked with and who are committed to mediated learning and unlocking the cognitive potential of all learners.

Publisher's Acknowledgments

Corwin Press gratefully acknowledges the contributions of the following reviewers of the first edition:

Kim Brown
Third-Grade Teacher
Scotland Accelerated Academy
Laurel Hill, NC

Katherine H. Greenberg
Professor of Educational Psychology
The University of Tennessee
Knoxville, TN

Maris Krasnow
Clinical Assistant Professor of
   Teaching and Learning
New York University
New York, NY

Paulette Mills
Associate Professor of
   Teaching and Learning
Washington State University
Pullman, WA

Lauren Mittermann
Seventh- and Eighth-Grade Social
   Studies Teacher
Gibraltar Middle School
Fish Creek, WI

Renee Peoples
Fourth-Grade Teacher
Swain West Elementary School
Bryson City, NC

Delise Teague
Instructional Coach
McNairy County Board
   of Education
Selmer, TN

About the Authors

Mandia Mentis is an Educational Psychologist and Senior Lecturer in the Special Education and Educational Psychology Programmes at Massey University, New Zealand. She is an accredited trainer of Feuerstein's Instrumental Enrichment (FIE) and the Learning Potential Assessment Device (LPAD) having completed her training at the International Centre for Learning Enhancement in Israel under Professor Feuerstein. Over the past 20 years, she has run Feuerstein's Instrumental Enrichment workshops with the Cognitive Research Centre in South Africa and with the Australasian Institute for Learning Enhancement in New Zealand. She has contributed extensively to research projects and publications and has co-written and published two books on Mediated Learning and Instrumental Enrichment. She has taught at primary, secondary, and college levels and has worked as an educational psychologist in both special and inclusive education settings. Her teaching and research interests include cognitive assessment, teaching for diversity, and e-learning. Her doctoral research focuses on developing effective e-learning communities of practice.

Marilyn Dunn-Bernstein's diverse career in education spans 36 years. Aside from her 20 years as a high school vice-principal, she has studied under Reuven Feuerstein and implemented the principles of structural cognitive modifiability, FIE, and MLE in an extensive range of educational settings. These included ten years of research, writing, and lecturing with the Cognitive Research Unit of the University of the Witwatersrand and 16 years of work with the Gifted Child Program for disadvantaged individuals in South African townships. Her current work as a psychologist in Australia involves enhancing cognitive, emotional, and creative development in autistic, Down's syndrome, Asperger's, and gifted individuals. She also works with undergraduate psychology and social sciences students and has been part of the team that runs Feuerstein workshops in Australia, New Zealand, and South Africa. She holds a PhD in Education, a master's in psychology, and a degree in human behavior.

Martene Mentis is an independent scholar, artist, and illustrator currently working as an art educator and graphic designer in New Zealand. She has many years of experience in education having taught in a variety of different settings. Her diverse educational background includes six years with the Cognitive Research Centre, University of the Witwatersrand, South Africa, where she contributed to research, lectured in Feuerstein's Instrumental Enrichment (FIE) workshops, and helped develop educational resources, including two books on Mediated Learning and Instrumental Enrichment. She completed her training in FIE under Professor Feuerstein, at the International Centre for Learning Enhancement in Israel, and in the Learning Potential Assessment Device (LPAD) at the Cognitive Research Centre in South Africa. She has an honor's degree in fine arts and a master's degree in education.

PART I

Metalearning

Structural Cognitive Modifiability

The human organism is open to modifiability at all ages and stages of development. Change is possible and desirable.

- Can intelligence be enhanced?

- Is our learning potential fixed?

- What role does genetics play in determining how we function in life?

- Can we overcome the negative conditions that poverty, emotional disturbances, and organic disorders have on learning?

- Does our past determine our future?

Part I attempts to answer these questions by outlining Feuerstein's theory of Structural Cognitive Modifiability (SCM) and introducing the concepts of passive acceptance and active modification.

Chapter 1

Unlocking Cognitive Potential

Feuerstein is well known for his work with students who struggle to learn. It is with the students who are considered lost, uneducable, or beyond change that Feuerstein has had his greatest success. Feuerstein's work with these students is based on his theory of Structural Cognitive Modifiability and the practices that support this theory.

THE THEORY OF STRUCTURAL COGNITIVE MODIFIABILITY

The theory of Structural Cognitive Modifiability (SCM) underpins Feuerstein's belief that individuals have the potential to change. It is helpful to focus on the three component parts of "modifiability" "cognitive," and "structural" to understand the approach that Feuerstein proposes.

1. Modifiability means having the ability to adapt, to alter, and to regulate.

2. Cognitive relates to the ability to think, reason, and learn.

3. Structural involves organization and integration of the components that make up our thinking.

In linking these three concepts together, Feuerstein encourages us to think of all learners as having the potential to change or adapt, and appropriately regulate the way they think, learn, and apply their skills in different contexts.

Feuerstein's approach is not aimed at trying to overcome a particular difficulty or teach a specific skill. Rather, it is aimed at teaching learners how to learn in order to adapt their learning for different situations. The change that Feuerstein wants to bring about is at a basic or structural level and the emphasis is on cognition. Behavior and emotions change as a result of cognitive changes, and these can overcome the negative influence of genetic predisposition, physical impairments, or educational deprivation.

Let's consider the following case study to see how this theory works in practice.

THE CASE OF M

> Eleven years ago, M was referred to the Feuerstein Institute for life-long placement in custodial care. At the time of his referral, he was 15-years-old and his IQ, according to the reports, was in the 35–44 range. His vocabulary consisted of 40–50 words and he manifested severe impairment of spatio-temporal orientation, imitation, retention, and social behavior. Echolalia (repetition of words) and echopraxia (repetition of movement) were observed, but no psychotic-autistic signs were detected. Trainability had been considered very poor, and custodial care seemed unavoidable.
>
> M was the second of three brothers. His father, a schizophrenic, alcoholic, and poorly adjusted Foreign Legion soldier, met and married M's mother in an Asian country. The mother was retarded and illiterate and died as a hospitalized, diagnosed psychotic. M suffered from brain damage caused by prematurity and low weight at birth and required prolonged incubator care. His infancy was marked by nutritional difficulties and by repeated and prolonged separations in nurseries and foster homes. His early adolescence was spent largely in socially and educationally restrictive environments (Feuerstein, 1980, p. 10).

Read the case of M again and respond to the following questions:

- What factors from this history do you think are important when considering M's situation?
- What do you think about M's intellectual level and his potential to achieve?
- What kind of intervention, placement, or teaching do you consider appropriate for M?
- How would you describe M's future?

Feuerstein believes that there are two approaches of looking at the case of M and responding to the questions above—a passive acceptance approach and an active modification approach.

A PASSIVE ACCEPTANCE APPROACH TO THE CASE OF M

A passive acceptance approach to answering the questions about M would focus on those aspects of M's history that include organic or innate factors—such as the father's alcoholism, the parents' mental disorders, M's premature birth, etc. These factors are all unchangeable—and can be seen as predicting a bleak future for M. His IQ score would be seen to be in the retarded range and this score will be interpreted as being fixed and static, thus limiting M's potential to achieve. Within this view, the only treatment would be to provide M with life placement in residential care, as he will not be able to function on his own. His future would be described as being very limited as, given his very low level of functioning, he will always be dependent on others.

In this approach, the past is seen as being a predictor of the future and a damaged past will predict a low level of functioning in the future. Intelligence is seen as being a fixed number, which is unchangeable. Treatment, then, is always to accommodate the low level of functioning that is presented. This view, according to Feuerstein, presents a very pessimistic view of our ability to learn because, as the term indicates, there is just a passive (without doing anything) acceptance and perpetuation of the status quo. There is no attempt to improve or change the low level of functioning, and arrangements are made to accommodate this low level of functioning through custodial care.

AN ACTIVE MODIFICATION
APPROACH TO THE CASE OF M

An active modification approach to answering the questions about M focuses on those aspects of M's past that can be changed—factors such as the restricted conditions that he lived in and being deprived of stimulation, language, and affection. These factors are all reversible—and so only present as a baseline for possible change. Within this approach, M's intelligence will be viewed as being dependent on the amount of stimulation he has had and there is a belief that, with intervention, M's intelligence can be improved. The treatment for M, then, would be intensive work in enrichment programs where M is taught how to learn. M's future would be described as being dependent on the amount that he is able to learn under stimulating conditions, and there would be hope that he would improve enough to live independently.

In the active modification approach, the past is seen as merely a starting point for improvements in the future. Intelligence is seen as being a propensity or tendency to adapt to new situations and hence is multidimensional, very complex, modifiable, and subject to change. Intervention then involves intensive stimulation and interaction aimed at teaching or mediating how to learn and adapt. This is a very optimistic view of the potential of all individuals to change and learn and, as the term indicates, involves actively trying to bring about change or modifiability.

> How did you answer the questions relating to the case of M? Did you focus more on passive acceptance issues or do you believe in active modification? What is your view of learning?

Feuerstein is firmly located in the active modification approach when working with learners who have difficulty. This is at the core of his theory of Structural Cognitive Modifiability. This theory proposes that with a belief in active modification, and using the tools of Mediated Learning Experience, we can bring about the necessary modification of the learners' cognitive dysfunctions, so that they can function as autonomous, independent individuals.

PASSIVE ACCEPTANCE AND ACTIVE MODIFICATION

Consider the actual outcome of the case of M as reported by Feuerstein.

> Contrary to all expectations, our assessment of M, using the Learning Potential Assessment Device, yielded a surprising level of modifiability. Accordingly, M was placed in a foster home, group care treatment program for the redevelopment of severely disturbed, low functioning adolescents. As a result of the intensive and concerted investment in M's development over the past 11 years, he has emerged as an independently functioning individual, oriented in space and time, with a full and rich command of spoken and written Hebrew, a sense of humor, social skills, and vocational ambitions. He is responsible for the maintenance of a large indoor swimming pool and has learned to speak French and some German.
>
> In spite of M's charged heredity, organic damage, maternal deprivation, and stimulus deprivation from his restricted early environments, all of which are considered responsible for retarded performance, he proved receptive to intervention, albeit of a sustained and systematic nature. The development of his capacity to use hierarchically higher levels of cognitive processes, such as representational, anticipatory and inferential thinking, to a large extent determined his general behavioral adaptations. Thus his entire destiny was changed from anticipated placement in life-long custodial care to the life of an autonomous, independent, adaptive young man, looking forward to building a future and starting a family. (Feuerstein, 1980, p. 10)

The case of M—as indeed many other real case studies—helps us to see the effects of Feuerstein's theory put into practice. The fact that M *did* change and that the change was significant, albeit over a long period of time with intensive intervention, is testament to Feuerstein's theory of Structural Cognitive Modifiability and his belief that change begets change through active modification.

Consider the following comparison of the two approaches—a passive acceptance approach and an active modification approach. Which approach fits with the actual outcome of the case of M? Which approach guides your practice?

Passive Acceptance	**Active Modification**
• A belief that humans are essentially unmodifiable and unchangeable	• A belief that human beings are flexible, open systems that have the potential to be modified
• A belief that an individual's future can be predicted on the basis of present and past levels of functioning	• A belief that individual's are open systems that have the potential to be modified
• A tendency to use "because of . . ." statements, e.g., "Because of his genetic problems he will not be able to . . ." or "Because his father was alcoholic he will be . . ."	• A tendency to use "in spite of statements, e.g., "In spite of his genetic problems he is motivated to change . . ."or "In spite of his mother's absence he is receptive to mediation . . ."statements
• A very pessimistic view	• A very optimistic view

This chapter covered Feuerstein's theory of Structural Cognitive Modifiability. This theory, based on Feuerstein's belief in active modification, holds that individuals can change the way they think and adapt to their world. This is an optimistic approach—if you believe there is a way, you will find a solution, irrespective of the difficulties that have come before. As in the case of M, despite the severe negative organic and situational factors that influenced his early life, a belief in active modification and SCM was the catalyst for Feuerstein to use the tools of Mediated Learning Experience and the Cognitive Map to bring about significant change in M. The next chapters will focus on these tools.

Feuerstein believes that the human organism is open to modifiability at all ages and stages of development and that change is possible and desirable.

What do you believe?

PART II

Metateaching

Mediated Learning Experience

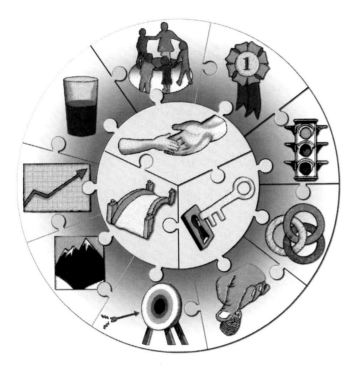

- How does learning occur?
- Why do some children develop effective thinking skills while others do not?
- What can parents and teachers do to help children learn from life experiences?

Part II attempts to answer these questions by discussing the theory and providing practical examples of what Feuerstein calls the Mediated Learning Experience (MLE).

> *The mediator enriches the interaction between the child and the environment with ingredients that do not pertain to the immediate situation but belong to a world of meanings and intentions derived from generations of culturally transmitted attitudes, values, goals, and means.*
>
> —Feuerstein, 1979

F euerstein believes that there are two modalities of learning—a direct approach and a mediated approach.

DIRECT APPROACH

The direct approach is based on Piaget's formula of S-O-R, which signifies that the organism (O), or individual learner, interacts directly with the stimuli (S) of the surrounding world and responds (R).

In this kind of interaction with the environment, learning is incidental. Consider the example of a child walking through a garden. The child directly interacts with the flowers and other stimuli. The child may smell the flowers, feel their texture, or even watch a bee settling on the flowers. While the kind of learning that takes place as a direct result of such experiences is fundamental and necessary, it is incidental and, according to Feuerstein, not enough to ensure that effective learning takes place.

MEDIATED APPROACH

Mediated learning is the second, and vital, approach, which ensures effective learning. Here, Feuerstein develops Piaget's formula of S-O-R further to include a human mediator between the world of stimuli, the organism, and the response. Feuerstein's new formula for mediated learning, then, is S-H-O-H-R, in which H is the human mediator. The mediator becomes interposed between the learning organism and the world of stimuli to interpret, guide, and give meaning to the stimuli. In this kind of interaction, learning is intentional.

Consider again the example of the child in the garden. If the mother were present as a mediator, she would focus the child's attention on specific stimuli and thereby interpret and give meaning to the child's encounter with the flowers. She could focus the child's attention on similar and different colors and textures, thereby teaching the child the important thinking skill of comparing. Or, she could interpret the bee's dance of pollination, thereby giving meaning to the bee's actions and showing the interconnections or relationships among stimuli. It is this kind of interaction, in which the mediator intervenes, that results in the child developing a predisposition to the type of learning that is prerequisite for proper cognitive functioning and adaptation to the world.

Both forms of exposure—direct and mediated—are necessary for optimal development. Feuerstein believes that it is mediated learning that allows a child to be more receptive to direct exposure and benefit more from it. This is because mediation is a type of interaction that develops the basic attitudes and competence for self-directed learning.

When a child does not interact effectively with the environment, or experiences difficulties with learning, we develop what Feuerstein calls a "stiff finger." Here, the index finger points stiffly in the direction of the child, indicating that the problem and failure is fixed firmly with the child. In mediation, however, learning is an interaction between the child and a mediator and fingers point in both directions.

12 CRITERIA OF MEDIATION

To date, Feuerstein has identified 12 criteria, or types of interaction, that are fundamental to mediation. He believes that the first three criteria are necessary and sufficient for an interaction to be considered mediation. The remaining nine criteria may function at different times where and when appropriate and serve to balance and reinforce each other. Mediation is a dynamic and open process and should not be rigidly applied or fixed at just 12 criteria.

The 12 criteria of mediation and their corresponding symbols are represented below.

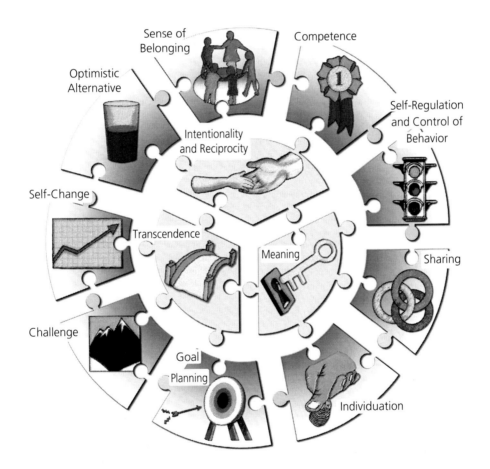

The relationship between MLE and the direct exposure modality of learning can be formulated as follows: the more a child has been afforded MLE and the more optimal the mediational process, the greater the capacity of the child to benefit and become modified by direct exposure to stimuli.

—Feuerstein, 1980, p. 16

THE AIM OF MEDIATED LEARNING

The aim of this part is to put Feuerstein's theory into practice by applying his criteria to various settings, namely, the classroom, the home, and the counseling/community situation. It should not be regarded as a "recipe book," but rather as a model or a process that describes how interaction can result in effective learning. The criteria are not necessarily new, but are concise and practical and can be applied in any setting with any subject matter. It has practical application and relevance for everyone involved in education.

The MLE approach allows anyone involved in a learning interaction to make the "stiff finger" more flexible and thus turn away from focusing on the child and point back and inward.

It should be noted that while the criteria and theory of MLE are based on Feuerstein's work, the elaboration and practical examples reflect our own interpretation and hence may deviate from Feuerstein and other interpretations of his theory.

Chapter 2

Intentionality and Reciprocity

Mediation of intentionality occurs when the mediator (e.g., parent, teacher, counselor) deliberately guides the interaction in a chosen direction by selecting, framing, and interpreting specific stimuli. Mediation is a purposeful and intentional act in which the mediator actively works to focus attention on the stimuli.

Reciprocity occurs when there is responsivity from the mediatee (learner) and an indication of being receptive to, and involved in, the learning process. The learner is open to the mediator's input and demonstrates cooperation.

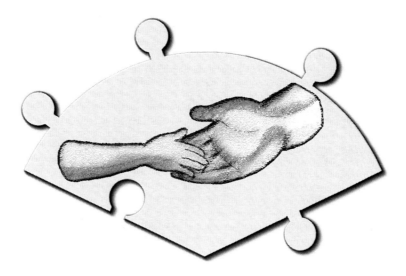

EXPLANATION

By offering a hand, the mediator invites the learner to engage with stimuli (intentionality). In reaching back, the learner's willingness to respond is communicated (reciprocity).

Mediation of intentionality and reciprocity is the first piece of the Mediated Learning Experience puzzle. To learn, we need to be able to create significance from the vast amount of stimuli that continually impact our senses. We need to isolate particular stimuli and interact with them. This is achieved through a reciprocal relationship between the mediator and the learner. The mediator isolates and interprets the stimuli (intentionality) and presents them in a manner that results in a response (reciprocity) from the learner.

Note

- Merely intending to intervene and interpret a stimulus will not guarantee that attention or vigilance will occur (e.g., writing a book does not ensure that it will be read).
- To ensure reciprocity, the mediator should actively seek the learner's attention and purposefully impose mediation (e.g., a reader must be drawn to open the book and actively engage in reading it).

In the Classroom

In some classroom situations, obstacles to intentionality and reciprocity may exist. For example, a teacher may wait for the child to initiate an interaction in the belief that it is important not to initiate the child's interaction with stimuli. In this case, there is no intentionality.

A second situation is one in which the teacher actively invites interaction in a well-prepared, relevant lesson but the students don't receive the initiation of the teacher because they are tired, lack interest or motivation, don't perceive the relevance of the given topic, or any other subjective reason. In this case, there is no reciprocity.

In the Home

Intentionality and reciprocity seem to begin naturally in the development of a child with the mother's need to interact with her newborn and to engage in eye contact with the child. The mother gradually directs the child's attention to objects like a rattle or a mobile. In so doing, she frames the stimulus for the child. This, in turn, creates in the child the ability to focus on the mother's face, to establish eye contact, and, with time, to engage in imitation and reciprocal smiling. Thus, the intentionality of the mother evokes the reciprocity of her child and vice versa.

This behavior can be contrasted with that of mediationally deprived children who do not receive consistent nurturing and, as a result, do not develop the ability to engage in reciprocal eye contact. As Feuerstein describes, their eyes slip off your face as if it were glass.

Remember

The three elements involved in and influencing intentionality and reciprocity are:

1. The mediator—whose language, pace, pitch, and gestures can be varied to enhance intentionality

2. The learner—whose attention span, interest level, and availability affect reciprocity

3. The stimulus (presentation of ideas and material)—which can be varied in terms of amplitude, repetition, modality, etc., to enhance both intentionality and reciprocity

---

Intentionality and reciprocity are the main conditions of an MLE interaction.

—Reuven Feuerstein

APPLICATION

Examples

In the Classroom

A teacher directs attention by framing a stimulus.

"Let's all gather closely around this picture. What colors are in the rainbow?"

Activities That Foster Mediation of Intentionality and Reciprocity

☐ The teacher arouses the students' interest and motivation in the subject matter and gets feedback from them.

☐ The students listen to and respond to the teacher in an atmosphere conducive to learning.

☐ The teacher reveals an interest in the students and their work, and shows pleasure when they succeed and make progress.

☐ The teacher is ready to reframe something that is not understood, and takes a special interest in slow learners and passive students.

☐ The teacher is well prepared and the classroom well organized, which communicates intentionality.

In the Home

A mother encourages interaction.

"Let's go play in the sandbox and see what we can make."

☐ The parent encourages the child to take an interest in the immediate environment and focuses the child's attention on a specific stimulus (an object, activity, or event).

☐ The caregiver displays an interest in the child and offers empathy and an understanding of events.

☐ The parent varies the approach to stimuli in order to meet the child's level of interest.

☐ The caregiver engages in eye contact and encourages the child to respond.

In the Counseling/ Community Situation

A therapist acknowledges involvement.

"Thank you for identifying those problem areas. Let's see what can be done to resolve them."

☐ The therapist invites collaboration from the client in developing therapy strategies.

☐ The counselor creates an atmosphere of concern by using an empathic listening approach.

☐ The therapist engages the client by modeling appropriate behavior.

☐ The community worker encourages introspection into problems and responds positively to ideas for their resolution.

MAKING LINKS

Mediation of intentionality and reciprocity can be linked to ideas and approaches that have been developed by others who are involved in education. Consider some of the following ideas from educationists, psychologists, and theorists that support and complement Feuerstein's ideas that teaching and learning are enhanced by mediating intentionality and reciprocity.

Reflect on the following views that link to mediation of intentionality and reciprocity:

There is, in fact, no teaching without learning. One requires the other.

—Paulo Freire

Education is not the filling of a bucket, rather, the lighting of a fire.

—William Butler Yeats

All of life is education and everybody is a teacher and everybody is forever a pupil.

—Abraham Maslow

Consider

Consider the work of the developmental psychologist L. S. Vygotsky (1896–1934) and his concept of the zone of proximal development (ZPD). Vygotsky (1987) defined the ZPD as "the distance between the actual developmental level as determined by independent problem solving and the level of potential development as determined through problem solving under adult guidance, or in collaboration with more capable peers" (p. 86). This relates to the gap between what learners can do by themselves and what they can achieve with the guidance of a teacher or someone mediating to them.

With the right kind of scaffolding or mediation, learners can be challenged to learn today what they could not achieve yesterday. They can be supported to attain what was previously just outside of their reach with the right kind of intervention. This relates well to Feuerstein's concept of intentionality and reciprocity, where with appropriate mediation (intentionality), a learner can be motivated to go that bit further than they are able to do if left to learn independently. The learner is ready to benefit from the mediation as it is pitched at the right level to extend understanding and develop skills. Working within the ZPD creates a conducive learning environment for the learner to be receptive. Vygotsky's concept of scaffolding learning within the ZPD complements Feuerstein's concept of intentionality and reciprocity:

Learning is only good when it proceeds ahead of development . . . [It then] awakens and rouses to life those functions which are in a stage of maturing.

—L. S. Vygotsky

Work Page ....

Think of your own understanding of how people learn. What other ideas, approaches, theories, or practices do you think link well with Feuerstein's concept of mediation of intentionality and reciprocity?

_____

_____

_____

_____

_____

_____

_____

_____

_____

_____

_____

_____

_____

_____

_____

_____

Work Page ·

This vignette illustrates an ineffectual, direct, and authoritarian approach often used in classrooms to maintain discipline and keep students busy.

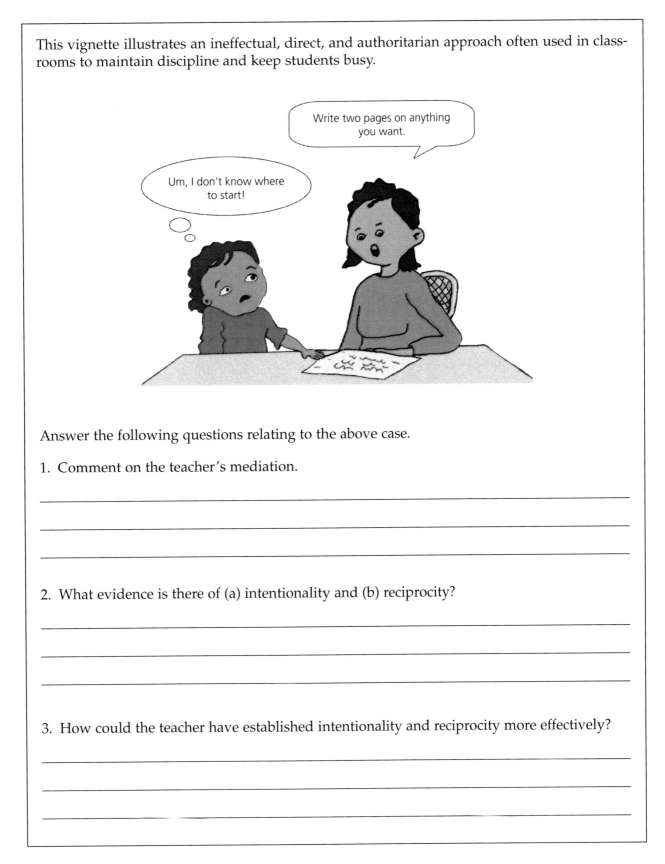

Answer the following questions relating to the above case.

1. Comment on the teacher's mediation.

_____

_____

_____

2. What evidence is there of (a) intentionality and (b) reciprocity?

_____

_____

_____

3. How could the teacher have established intentionality and reciprocity more effectively?

_____

_____

_____

Work Page ....

True or False

Write **T** below the true statements and **F** below the false statements.

1. Intentionality and reciprocity are two sides of the same coin. Essentially, they are the deliberate intention of the mediator to focus the learner/child and elicit a willingness to participate in the learning situation. _____

2. Intentionality always occurs when the mediator comes to the classroom well prepared. _____

Define

Define *intentionality* and *reciprocity* in your own words.

_____

_____

_____

_____

Modify

Replace the following statement with one that would improve the mediation of intentionality and reciprocity.

"Get out your books and start working."

_____

_____

_____

_____

Think About

Educators of the Montessori method believe that children should be allowed to experiment freely with stimuli and that the teacher should follow the child and wait for the child to ask for an explanation. Do you think this contradicts intentionality and reciprocity?

_____

_____

_____

_____

Chapter 3

Meaning

Mediation of meaning occurs when the mediator conveys the significance and purpose of an activity. The mediator shows interest and emotional involvement, discusses the importance of the activity with the learner, and elicits an understanding of why the activity should be done.

EXPLANATION

It is as if the mediator provides a key to understanding the significance of stimuli. The key, or the mediation of meaning, unlocks and interprets the cultural context in which the mediatee is situated.

Mediation of meaning is the second piece of the Mediated Learning Experience puzzle. The first piece of the puzzle, the mediation of intentionality and reciprocity, is concerned with selecting and framing an activity or object. Mediation of meaning is concerned with charging that activity or object with value and energy, which makes it relevant to the learner.

The process of investing stimuli with meaning often involves communicating ethical and social values. Mediation of meaning is "the process by which knowledge, values and beliefs are transmitted from one generation to the next" (Feuerstein, 1980, p. 13).

Note

Meaning is mediated by investing significance at both the cognitive (intellectual) and affective (emotional) levels:

- Values and beliefs are communicated at the cognitive level.
- Energy and enthusiasm are communicated at the affective level.

In the Home

A caregiver mediates intentionality and reciprocity when preparing a bath for the child by running the water and helping him or her get undressed. The caregiver mediates meaning by encouraging enjoyment of the water and providing reasons for the bath experience. In this way, he or she helps the child get excited about the activity and understand its significance.

In response to critics who ask what right mediators have to impose their values on the learner, Feuerstein in turn asks what right have they not to. Consider the following:

- When a mother gives meaning to everything she does, the child begins to want and need meaning in all aspects of life.
- The process of investing meaning stimulates the child to ask questions and sets the basis for all further inquiry, future challenge, and possible rejection of that meaning.

- Without a firm understanding of the environment, a child is not empowered to respond to it—either to accept it or to transform it.
- Without mediation of meaning, the child is deprived of access to cognitively and affectively enriched stimuli.

For these reasons, Feuerstein believes it is every mediatee's right to receive Mediated Learning Experiences and the mediator's duty to provide them.

Although mediators may choose not to consciously impose their values on the mediatee, it is inevitable for this process to occur to some degree. No situation is value free. However, if the mediation of meaning is not explicit, the mediatee's ability to perceive meaning as being value laden and to critically evaluate situations is reduced.

> *Meaning is the emotional and energetic principle that requires mediators to ensure that the stimulus they are presenting to children gets through. It is the needle that carries the thread through the cloth.*
>
> —H. Sharron

APPLICATION

Examples

In the Classroom

The teacher motivates the lesson.

"We are studying geography in order to understand the physical world we live in."

Activities That Foster Mediation of Meaning

☐ The teacher conveys the importance or value of various subjects to the students.

☐ The teacher makes explicit the underlying strategies and skills involved in a task.

☐ The teacher energizes stimuli by changing their frequency and/or intensity.

☐ The teacher uses nonverbal behavior (position, facial expression, level, and inflection of voice) to convey meaning.

☐ The teacher acknowledges the meaning expressed by the students' responses.

In the Home

The caregiver transmits value.

"We are grateful for rain because we need water to live."

☐ The parent explains the reason why certain restrictions are imposed on behavior.

☐ The parent conveys the importance of activities through modeling behavior.

☐ The parent verbalizes his or her reasons for carrying out daily activities while doing them.

☐ The mother encourages the child to seek meaning in order to understand his or her environment.

☐ The caregiver shares the underlying significance of cultural events.

In the Counseling/ Community Situation

A therapist justifies an assessment.

"We are testing you to see what things are easy or difficult for you; then we will know how best to help you."

☐ The therapist conveys the importance of appropriate behavior in certain situations.

☐ The counselor helps the client make explicit his or her value system.

☐ The social worker discusses the relevance and value of a particular project and promotes enthusiasm for participating in community functions.

☐ The therapist interprets and reflects the feelings of his or her client.

MAKING LINKS

Mediation of meaning can be linked to ideas and approaches that have been developed by others who are involved in education. Consider some of the following ideas from educationists, psychologists, and theorists that support and complement Feuerstein's idea that teaching and learning are enhanced by mediating meaning.

Reflect on the following views that link to mediation of meaning:

He who has a "why" to live for can bear with almost any "how."

—Friedrich Nietzsche

The important thing is not to stop questioning.

—Albert Einstein

To have an aim is to act with meaning.

—John Dewey

Consider

Consider the work of the psychologist Viktor Frankl (1905–1997), who suffered the horrors of the Holocaust and throughout his terrible experience came to realize that the people who had any chance of surviving the Nazi death camps were the people that had hope for a future and believed that there was a reason or purpose for living and suffering. Frankl's philosophy was that life has meaning no matter what the circumstances and that people have the ability to find that meaning. This philosophy is outlined in his book *Man's Search for Meaning,* and from this he developed a form of therapy called logotherapy. Logotherapy comes from the Greek word "logos" which translates as "that which gives reason for being." Finding a purpose in life's experiences is central to logotherapy. This concept resonates with the Feuersteinian approach of mediating meaning, which invests significance and value in what is being learnt.

For the meaning of life differs from man to man, from day to day and from hour to hour. What matters, therefore, is not the meaning of life in general but rather the specific meaning of a person's life at a given moment.

—Frankl, 1985, p. 130

Work Page ·

Think of your own understanding of learning. What other ideas, approaches, theories, or practices can you link with Feuerstein's concept of mediation of meaning?

_____

_____

_____

_____

_____

_____

_____

_____

_____

_____

_____

_____

_____

_____

_____

_____

_____

_____

Work Page ....

Often, as parents, we transmit messages to our children without investing the content with some meaning that is relevant to the child.

Answer the following questions relating to the above vignette.

1. How do you think Alex's father failed to mediate meaning to Alex in this scenario?

_____

_____

_____

2. Cite an example of how Alex's father could have mediated meaning.

_____

_____

_____

3. Could intentionality and reciprocity also be used to solve the communication breakdown between the father and the son?

_____

_____

_____

Work Page ....

True or False

Write **T** below the true statements and **F** below the false statements.

1. Mediation of meaning involves giving reasons for actions. _____

2. A child's understanding of his or her world is established through the mediator's explanation of situations. _____

Define

Define *mediation of meaning* in your own words.

_____

_____

_____

_____

Modify

Replace the following statement with one that would improve the mediation of meaning.

"Don't bully!"

_____

_____

_____

_____

Think About

In the 1960s, it was believed that parents and teachers did not have the right to impose their values on children by mediating meaning and that foisting a preconceived meaning on a stimulus was indoctrination. What do you think?

_____

_____

_____

_____

Chapter 4

Transcendence

Mediation of transcendence occurs when an interaction goes beyond the immediate and direct need, thereby enlarging and diversifying the need system of the learner. The goal of mediating transcendence is to promote the acquisition of principles, concepts, or strategies that can be generalized to issues beyond the present problem.

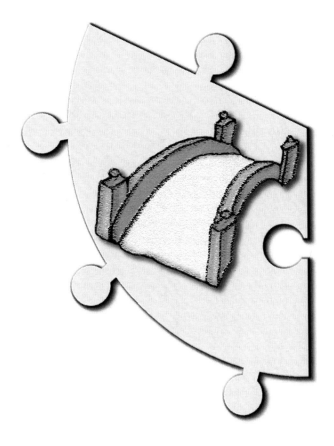

EXPLANATION

Every single activity has in it the potential for transcendence. Transcendence is the bridge that connects related activities and ideas, and links immediate needs to ever expanding needs.

Mediation of transcendence is the third piece of the Mediated Learning Experience puzzle, and transcendence is the third essential criterion for rendering an interaction a Mediated Learning Experience. In essence, any act that is a Mediated Learning Experience must include intentionality and reciprocity, meaning, and transcendence.

Mediation of transcendence occurs when the mediator links a specific issue or activity with others. This moves the learner beyond the direct and immediate need elicited by an interaction and bridges it to related issues and activities. In doing so, the mediator enlarges the need system of the mediatee to include the need for understanding, reflective thinking, and forming relationships among things.

Transcendence develops in the child (1) a deeper understanding of the world, (2) a perception of how things are interconnected, (3) a curiosity to inquire and discover relationships among things, and (4) a desire to know more about things and seek explanations.

In the Classroom

In the classroom, the potential for transcendence is limited when the focus is on facts and rote regurgitation of those facts, and when knowledge is fragmented and compartmentalized.

This potential can be realized when the focus is on process teaching—the teaching of underlying skills—and when knowledge is integrated and linked to a broader context.

In the Home

Transcendence in the home is limited when no explanations are given for actions and when no connections are drawn between events. However, when links are made to related events, the mediator transcends the superficial goal.

For example, a mundane trip to the supermarket could move beyond the immediate need of buying groceries by engaging in a discussion about

- Where products come from
- How products are grown and packaged
- Why products are displayed in various categories

- What different products cost and reveal about the value of money
- How advertising influences our choice of products
- How certain products impact the environment

Remember

Mediation of transcendence involves

- Finding a general rule that applies to related situations
- Linking events in the present with future and past events
- Engaging in reflective thinking to reach an underlying understanding of a situation
- Thinking laterally about experiences and issues

> *Education is what survives when what has been learned has been forgotten.*
>
> —B. F. Skinner

APPLICATION

Examples

In the Classroom

A teacher elicits the underlying principle.

"What rule can you generate from the spelling of niece, piece, receipt, and deceive?"

Activities That Would Foster Mediation of Transcendence

- ☐ The teacher connects the subject of the lesson to previous or future subjects.
- ☐ The teacher reveals the relationship between specific content and general goals.
- ☐ The teacher prefers "why" and "how" questions to "who" and "what" questions.
- ☐ The teacher generalizes and asks the students to generalize from specific instances to the underlying rule.
- ☐ The teacher evokes the students' need to seek and find complex relationships by providing bridging examples.

In the Home

A parent encourages generalization.

"Look at this red flower. What other things can we find that are the same color?"

- ☐ The parent models a particular behavior and explains to the child its appropriateness in a variety of situations.
- ☐ The mother provides the child with the vocabulary to enable a link to related concepts.
- ☐ The father encourages the child to relate a new experience to previously acquired concepts or ideas.
- ☐ The caregiver stimulates the child to explore beyond the immediate experience, thereby enlarging the child's understanding of the environment.

In the Counseling/ Community Situation

The therapist links skills gained in therapy to everyday situations.

"We have discussed the principles of effective communication; now try them at home."

- ☐ The therapist works on role play within the therapy situation, then asks the client to try the same behavior at home.
- ☐ The counselor connects seemingly disparate problems by examining their common cause.
- ☐ The community worker facilitates insight into community systems that can be applied to family dynamics.
- ☐ The therapist links present difficulties to past experiences in order to generate alternative solutions.
- ☐ The counselor interprets a child's problems in terms of family interactions.

MAKING LINKS

Mediation of transcendence can be linked to ideas and approaches that have been developed by others who are involved in education. Consider some of the following ideas from educationists, psychologists and theorists that support and complement Feuerstein's ideas that teaching and learning are enhanced by mediating transcendence.

> Reflect on the following views that link to mediation of transcendence:
>
> *Mere mechanical memorization of the superficial aspects of the object is not true learning.*
>
> —Paulo Freire
>
> *If you study to remember, you will forget, but, if you study to understand, you will remember.*
>
> —Anonymous

Consider

Consider the views of the cognitive psychologist Robert Sternberg who believed that an intelligent person is someone who is able to balance three kinds of skills: analytical skills (analyzing and contrasting things), creative skills (inventing and discovering things), and practical skills (applying skills in practice). He called this the Triarchic Theory of intelligence (Sternberg, 1988) and said that intelligence involves balancing these three skills to suit the context or environment. Intelligent learning is not about remembering facts and information, but rather being able to analyze and evaluate information and think about it creatively in order to apply it in different situations in ways that are appropriate for that situation. This view of intelligent learning is quite similar to Feuerstein's view of the importance of mediating transcendence. Both involve going beyond the here and now to underlying principles so that learners can apply what they have learned in different contexts. By exploring the work of various theorists in this text, we are transcending the views of Feuerstein's mediated learning.

Rudyard Kipling also highlights—in a humorous way—the importance of developing thinking skills for transcendence.

> *I keep six honest serving-men*
> *(They taught me all I knew);*
> *Their names are What and Why and When*
> *And How and Where and Who.*
>
> —Rudyard Kipling,
> "The Elephant's Child" in *Just So Stories*

Work Page ·

Think of your own understanding of learning. What other ideas, approaches, theories, or practices can you link with Feuerstein's concept of mediation of transcendence?

_____

_____

_____

_____

_____

_____

_____

_____

_____

_____

_____

_____

_____

_____

_____

_____

_____

_____

Work Page ········· · · · · · ·

One of the primary roles of a counselor is to empower the client by helping them "bridge" the strategies discussed in counseling to the outside world where the individual must function.

Answer the following questions relating to this vignette.

1. How does the counselor mediate transcendence to Kylie?

_____

_____

_____

2. Comment on the effectiveness of using this approach in counseling.

_____

_____

_____

3. What other opportunities are there in this scenario for the counselor to mediate transcendence?

_____

_____

_____

Work Page ·························

True or False

Write **T** below the true statements and **F** below the false statements.

1. The parent mediates transcendence when in response to a simple question he or she provides more than the child asked for. _____

2. Encouraging the student to find relationships among events is a form of mediating transcendence. _____

Define

Define *transcendence* in your own words.

_____

_____

_____

_____

Modify

Replace the following statement with one that would improve the mediation of transcendence.

"We are studying this part of history because it is a high school graduation requirement."

_____

_____

_____

_____

Think About

Teachers are often bound by a syllabus and believe that it is their responsibility to ensure that students pass their exams. As a result, they refrain from engaging in activities that are not part of the syllabus and, thereby, fail to mediate transcendence. They believe that linking the present subject matter to other topics or life experiences might distract the students. What do you think?

_____

_____

_____

_____

Chapter 5

Competence

Mediation of competence occurs when the mediator helps the learner develop the self-confidence to engage successfully in a given act. It is not necessarily the outcome of success that is important, but rather the learner's perception of it.

EXPLANATION

The feeling of competence is not necessarily associated with an objective or an absolute definition of success, but rather with the learner's perception of having been successful. It can be likened to the learner's ability to pin a mental medal on himself for a task done well.

Mediation of competence is the fourth piece of the Mediated Learning Experience puzzle. It involves developing the learner's self-confidence. Self-confidence is empowering; it facilitates independent thought, encourages motivated action, and contributes to the realization of goals. As such, mediation of competence is an invaluable component of any Mediated Learning Experience.

Competence should be seen in neither absolute terms nor as an innate ability or deficiency, but rather as a process. Competence on a task improves with experience and maturity.

Mediating competence involves instilling in the learner

- A good mental set
- A positive belief in his or her ability
- The motivation to try
- The determination to persevere

Ways in which competence can be mediated include

- Selecting stimuli within the level of expertise of the learner
- Rewarding the learner's response to the stimulus
- Making explicit the strategies used by the learner that result in a successful experience
- Focusing on and making explicit successfully completed parts of an activity, even though the whole activity might be unsuccessful

In the Classroom

Confidence can be eroded easily in the classroom. Educational systems that are competitive and product-oriented often focus more attention on errors than on the steps toward success. When negative attention is directed toward mistakes, students begin to define themselves in terms of their weaknesses rather than in terms of their strengths. This negative perception leads to the type of self-image in which the child believes that he or she is never good enough, irrespective of his or her achievements.

A poor self-image can be responsible for a variety of behavioral problems in the classroom, such as

- Lack of confidence, where students become so concerned with the perceived superior ability of teachers and peers that they are reluctant to attempt or persevere with tasks
- Lack of motivation, where students avoid or opt out of tasks
- Anxiety, resulting in impulsivity and erratic performance

The perceptions that parents and teachers have of children and convey to them, both explicitly and implicitly, have a profound impact on their sense of competence. Children often live up (or down) to others' expectations, resulting in a self-fulfilling prophecy.

Remember

The various components of the Mediated Learning Experience should not be seen in isolation. All 12 pieces of the Mediated Learning Experience puzzle complement and balance each other.

For example, the mediation of competence, as a process toward success, reinforces the mediation of self-change, or the perception of inner growth and progress (see Chapter 11).

Perhaps the most important single cause of a person's success or failure educationally has to do with the question of what he believes about himself.

—Arthur W. Combs

APPLICATION

Examples

In the Classroom

The teacher praises.

"You've done very well on this math problem."

Activities That Foster Mediation of Competence

☐ The teacher modifies the stimuli according to the students' level of competence by selecting appropriate material, simplifying, slowing down, and repeating.

☐ The teacher phrases questions according to the students' level of development.

☐ The teacher interprets the reasons for the students' success, and makes sure they understand the processes that lead to successful performance.

☐ The teacher makes the students aware of their progress.

☐ The teacher responds to positive elements in the students' work, even when the overall results are unsatisfactory.

In the Home

The mother gives reasons for the child's success.

"Well done! This time you held the cup with both hands and you didn't spill any of the milk."

☐ The father focuses on the child's good behavior rather than on the bad.

☐ The mother does chores with the child's "help" and shows her appreciation.

☐ The parent praises the child for applying problem-solving strategies successfully.

☐ The caregiver takes the child's level of development into account when structuring an activity.

☐ The parent encourages the child to recognize the reasons underlying successful behavior.

In the Counseling/ Community Situation

The community worker praises and reflects on successful intervention.

"Your empathy for children enabled you to settle the dispute effectively."

☐ The counselor works through strengths in order to remediate weaknesses, thus ensuring a feeling of competence.

☐ The community worker empowers the group members by identifying their particular talents or skills.

☐ The therapist helps the child represent progress on a chart.

☐ The counselor breaks down a difficult concept in order to make it accessible.

MAKING LINKS

Mediation of competence can be linked to ideas and approaches that have been developed by others who are involved in education. Consider some of the following ideas from educationists, psychologists and theorists that support and complement Feuerstein's ideas that teaching and learning are enhanced by mediating competence.

Reflect on the following views that link to mediation of competence:

There is no better way to teach your children that they are valuable people than by valuing them. The more children feel valuable, the more they will then begin to say things of value. They will rise to your experience of them.

—M. Scott Peck

Self-belief does not necessarily ensure success, but self-disbelief assuredly spawns failure.

—Albert Bandura

Education is helping the child realise his potentialities.

—Erich Fromm

Consider

Consider the work of the social psychologist Albert Bandura, whose social cognitive theory highlighted the importance in learning on focusing on what people believed about their ability to perform. He developed the notion of self-efficacy and showed how what learners think and feel about themselves influences how they are motivated to behave. Learners who have a positive belief about their ability to succeed, and their competence, are able to accomplish things more easily and feel better about themselves. They are also more likely to face challenges that are difficult and persevere with them rather than try and avoid these situations. A strong self-efficacy, or sense of competence, enables a learner to spring back from failure more effectively. The learners believe that overcoming failure, by acquiring more skills or knowledge, is in their control. Self-efficacy is achieved through having successful experiences, watching positive role models, being reassured after failure, and being persuaded to try again. This approach seems to complement Feuerstein's notion of mediation of competence where instilling a belief in the ability to be successful enhances one's ability to learn.

People who have a sense of self efficacy bounce back from failures; they approach things in terms of how to handle them rather than worrying about what can go wrong.

—Albert Bandura

Work Page ....

Think of your own understanding of how people learn. What other ideas, approaches, theories, or practices do you think link well with Feuerstein's concept of mediation of competence?

_____

_____

_____

_____

_____

_____

_____

_____

_____

_____

_____

_____

_____

_____

_____

_____

_____

Work Page ·····················

In sheer frustration, a teacher may hand back a test that reflects no learning on behalf of the student and the teacher is forced to comment!

Answer the following questions relating to the above case.

1. Comment on whether you think mediation of competence is shown in the above scenario.

_____

_____

_____

2. What evidence is there that negative labeling has occurred? What impact does this have on Juanita?

_____

_____

_____

3. What approach could the teacher have taken in handing back a poor test result to Juanita?

_____

_____

_____

Work Page ....

True or False

Write **T** below the true statements and **F** below the false statements.

1. The therapist who provides the low-functioning child with a realistic assessment of his or her weaknesses is mediating competence. _____

2. The teacher should take the students' developmental levels into account when planning activities. _____

Define

Define *competence* in your own words.

_____

_____

_____

_____

Modify

Replace the following statement with one that would improve the mediation of competence.

"This essay is just as bad as last time—is it really worth you trying a rewrite?"

_____

_____

_____

_____

Think About

Our current educational system equates success with getting the right end product. Therefore, rewarding a child for the positive aspects of his or her working process, even when the end product is unsuccessful, is doing the child a disservice because this approach to learning is incompatible with the existing system. What do you think?

_____

_____

_____

_____

Chapter 6

Self-Regulation and Control of Behavior

Mediation of self-regulation and control of behavior occurs when the mediator intervenes in order to make the learner conscious of the need to self-monitor and adjust behavior. The rapidity and intensity of the mental activity is modified according to the characteristics of the stimuli and the circumstances.

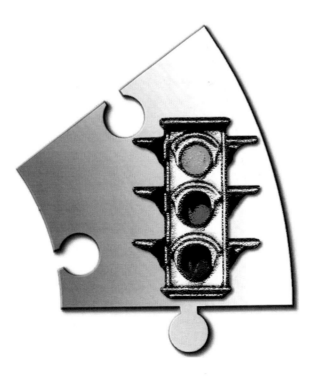

EXPLANATION

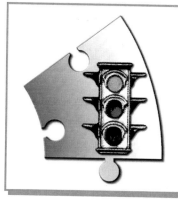

Mediating self-regulation and control of behavior can be likened to instilling in a child a self-regulatory traffic light. The red light will stop the child from rushing impulsively into a task or situation, the yellow light will caution the child to engage in reflective thinking about the task, and the green light will encourage the child to go through the activity systematically and appropriately.

Mediation of self-regulation and control of behavior is the fifth piece of the Mediated Learning Experience puzzle. Its aim is to encourage children to take responsibility for their own learning and behavior. It involves teaching children to think about their own thinking (metacognition) and behavior and to choose appropriate responses to a particular stimulus or situation. When we dictate to children how to respond and structure their reactions in a situation, we decrease their chances for autonomy and self-monitoring.

Mediation of self-regulation and control of behavior involve helping the child to analyze a task in order to adjust his or her behavior appropriately. For example, a common or familiar task can be executed more quickly than a novel task, and an easy activity requires less effort than a complicated one. Adjusting behavior in response to the particular circumstances of the task involves (1) restraining impulsivity; (2) breaking down complex problems into smaller parts; and (3) engaging in a systematic approach rather than wild guessing.

In the Classroom

The following examples demonstrate the mediation of metacognition in two different educational settings.

Elementary school students were asked to focus on ways of controlling their impulsivity. Following an explanation of Feuerstein's motto of "just a moment, let me think" and the traffic light image, they were asked to generate their own self-regulatory approach. The class unanimously accepted the motto "Think before you ink" as their reminder to engage in metacognition.

A group of high school students were told to act as their own teacher by providing written comments that evaluated an assignment. Initially this proved to be an exceptionally difficult task for the students, who were used to being passively dependent on their teacher for assessments of performance. However, as they became more actively aware of their own learning processes they were able to independently assess the reasons for their success or failure and hence monitor and adjust their own response to a task.

Remember

Mediating self-regulation and control of behavior should be linked to other pieces of the Mediated Learning Experience puzzle. For example, in order to shift the focus of the learner from one of being a passive recipient of information to one of being an active, independent, and autonomous learner, the mediation of self-regulation and control of behavior can be combined with mediating

- Competence—where the student's perception of success enables him or her to take responsibility for his or her own learning (see Chapter 5)
- Goal planning—where envisaging a goal encourages the student to plan and undertake the necessary steps to achieve it (see Chapter 9)
- Self-change—where the student becomes aware of progress by monitoring behavior (see Chapter 11)

Man's self-concept is enhanced when he takes responsibility for himself.

—William C. Shutz

APPLICATION

Examples

In the Classroom

To guard against impulsivity, the class motto is,

"Wait a minute; let me think."

Activities That Foster the Mediation of Self-Regulation and Control of Behavior

- ☐ The teacher emphasizes self-discipline.
- ☐ The teacher models regulated and controlled behavior by not interrupting student answers, reflecting before answering, admitting his or her own impulsivity, and structuring the lesson.
- ☐ The teacher assists students in regulating behavior by asking them to concentrate on certain subjects, reread paragraphs, think before answering, and check their own work.
- ☐ The teacher encourages students to organize work and plan according to priority.
- ☐ The teacher talks through the solution to problems in order to demonstrate a strategy.
- ☐ The teacher allows students to evaluate their own work as if they were the teacher.

In the Home

The parent helps the child respond appropriately.

"How can we cross this street safely?"

- ☐ The parent demonstrates that rushing into tasks without prior planning reduces the chances of success.
- ☐ The father identifies the steps involved in a complex task that he and the child are completing together.
- ☐ The caregiver models how easy and familiar tasks can be completed quickly while more difficult and complicated tasks require more careful planning.
- ☐ The parent fosters the child's awareness of the consequences of actions and the need to take responsibility for them.

In the Counseling/ Community Situation

The therapist encourages reflective action rather than impulsive reaction.

"Rather than just reacting to your partner's demands, think about a strategy for effective communication."

- ☐ The community worker models careful analysis of a problem as opposed to rushing to quick and easy solutions.
- ☐ The therapist guides the client to recognize the build-up of emotions that lead to antisocial behavior and the steps needed for its control.
- ☐ The community worker elicits from the group the process by which they solved a problem in order to facilitate taking responsibility for their actions.
- ☐ The therapist helps the client plan a study timetable.

MAKING LINKS

Mediation of self-regulation and control of behavior can be linked to ideas and approaches that have been developed by others who are involved in education. Consider some of the following ideas from educationists, psychologists, and theorists that support and complement Feuerstein's ideas that teaching and learning are enhanced by mediating self-regulation and control of behavior.

Reflect on the following views that link to mediation of a sense of self-regulation and control of behavior:

We need to be the authors of our own life.

—Peter Senge

Unless you know everything, what you need is thinking.

—Edward de Bono

For a person to feel responsible for his actions, he must sense that the behaviour has flowed from the self.

—Stanley Milgram

The individual who sees himself and his situation clearly and who freely takes responsibility for that self and for that situation is a very different person from one who is simply in the grip of outside circumstances.

—Carl Rogers

Consider

Consider the concept of metacognition first introduced by the developmental psychologist John Flavell (1979). According to Flavell, metacognition involves both metacognitive knowledge (knowing about how we think and learn) and metacognitive regulation (being able to manage our learning). Metacognition can thus be described as "thinking about thinking," "knowing about knowing" or "controlling learning." Successful learners are those who are aware of their learning and can monitor and change their learning as appropriate. They are in control by being able to self-assess and self-manage through having a plan, monitoring the plan, and evaluating the plan. In the self-assessment *planning stage,* the learner will decide what prior learning will help with the new task and the best method to problem solve in the new context. In the *monitoring phase,* the learner will examine how the task is progressing and whether something different needs to be done. In the *evaluation phase,* the leaner will consider how well the task turned out and whether there is new learning to be done. Metacognition complements Feuerstein's notion of mediation of a self-regulation and control of behavior, where effective learning occurs when the learner manages his or her own learning process.

What then can be the purport of the injunction, know thyself? I suppose it is that the mind should reflect upon itself.

—Augustine, De Trinitate

Work Page ....

Think of your own understanding of how people learn. What other ideas, approaches, theories, or practices do you think link well with Feuerstein's concept of mediation of a sense of self-regulation and control of behavior?

_____

_____

_____

_____

_____

_____

_____

_____

_____

_____

_____

_____

_____

_____

_____

_____

_____

Work Page ....

Often a child's poor behavior or lack of control in stressful situations is a direct result of just not knowing how to self-manage. This can be mediated.

Answer the following questions relating to the above case.

1. Has the mother modeled an attitude that promotes effective self-regulation and control of behavior?

_____

_____

_____

2. Comment on Shimon's ability to self-regulate.

_____

_____

_____

3. Give other examples of how the mother could mediate self-regulation and control of behavior in this scenario.

_____

_____

_____

Work Page ....

True or False

Write **T** below the true statements and **F** below the false statements.

1. The therapist who uses professional expertise to provide immediate solutions to the client's problem is mediating regulation of behavior. _____

2. The student who checks answers before handing in an exam is demonstrating self-regulation and control of behavior. _____

Define

Define *self-regulation* and *control of behavior* in your own words.

_____

_____

_____

_____

Modify

Replace the following statement with one that would improve the mediation of self-regulation and control of behavior.

"Redo! This work is full of careless errors."

_____

_____

_____

_____

Think About

Spontaneity and impulsivity are often seen to be at the heart of creativity. Mediating self-regulation and control of behavior involves restraining impulsivity and engaging in systematic and planned, rather than spontaneous, behavior. Therefore, mediation of self-regulation and control of behavior could stifle creativity. What do you think?

_____

_____

_____

_____

Chapter 7

Sharing

Mediation of sharing behavior relates to the interdependence of the mediator and the learner and of individuals in general. It is the mutual need for cooperation at a cognitive and affective level. Sharing develops empathy through social interaction.

EXPLANATION

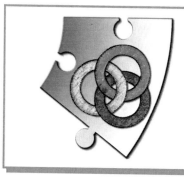

Sharing relates to the intrinsic need for interdependence. It can be likened to interlocking circles that together explore and share in the learning situation, but at the same time maintain their characteristics of individuality.

Mediation of sharing behavior is the sixth piece of the Mediated Learning Experience puzzle. It concerns a person's need to connect with others. Feuerstein believes it is "one of the foundations of our social existence" (as cited in Sharron, 1987, p. 17).

Mediation of sharing occurs when the mediator and learner, or a group of learners, focus on an activity together and respond together. The mediator shares ideas and feelings and encourages the learner to do the same. Sharing is the reciprocal need for cooperation at both an intellectual and emotional level. It involves openly listening to another point of view and being sensitive to the feelings of others.

Mediation of sharing emphasizes cooperation; the result is to promote competence in social interactions by way of the following:

- Environment of trust is developed with mutual self-disclosure
- Self-concept is strengthened when successes are shared and failures are worked through with an empathic listener
- Sharing ideas both verbally and in written form helps develop cognitive processes and clarify confused thinking

In the Classroom

While mediation of sharing behavior is automatically part of any healthy family, it is often ignored or even discouraged in some classrooms. In the traditional classroom, in which the teacher dominates and directs the teaching to the class as a whole, the students become isolated and passive. As a result, student-to-student interactions are minimal and learning is individualistic and competitive.

In order to deemphasize competitive learning in the classroom and, instead, mediate sharing behavior, more cooperative learning can be introduced. This includes group work, peer tutoring, and an emphasis on students as active and social learners rather than passive recipients of teaching.

In the Home

Sharing behavior begins in the womb as a mother shares her body with the fetus. The close emotional bond between child and parent is nurtured through eye contact, and pointing at and playing together with objects. It develops into "give-and-take" interactions, empathic communication, and sophisticated social relationships.

Sharing can be mediated in the home by encouraging turn-taking and cooperation. Sharing the day's events over the dinner table and helping with household chores not only strengthen family relationships but also facilitate the development of social skills.

Remember

All the criteria of mediated learning balance and complement each other. For example, sharing, where interdependence is promoted, is constantly balanced with individuation, where independence of action and thought is encouraged (see Chapter 8).

> *There is no self without others.*
>
> —Anonymous

APPLICATION

Examples

In the Classroom

The teacher facilitates interaction.

"Would you and Sue discuss the question and then tell the class your answer?"

Activities That Foster the Mediation of Sharing Behavior

☐ The teacher encourages students to help and listen to each other. The teacher instills in the students sensitivity toward others.
☐ The teacher arranges opportunities for group activities. The teacher selects subject matter that emphasizes the importance of cooperation.
☐ The teacher applies group-teaching methods and encourages the students to share their experience with others.

In the Home

The father encourages the child to relate his or her experiences.

"Tell me about your day at the zoo with Granny."

☐ The mother facilitates cooperation among family members by encouraging turn-taking and promoting the sharing of chores.
☐ The parent models sharing behavior by relating experiences to his or her children and allowing them to share their feelings.
☐ The caregiver arranges opportunities for participation in play groups and other group activities.

In the Counseling/ Community Situation

The counselor fosters cooperation.

"Problems are often a lot less complicated if faced together—two heads are better than one."

☐ The therapist encourages clients to share their problems, seeking commonality with each other and developing support groups.
☐ The therapist models empathic listening in a group-therapy setting.
☐ The counselor allows the group to experience the benefits of a democratic approach.
☐ The community worker initiates discussion about the benefits of sharing rather than competing for scarce resources.

MAKING LINKS

Mediation of sharing can be linked to ideas and approaches that have been developed by others who are involved in education. Consider some of the following ideas from educationists, psychologists, and theorists that support and complement Feuerstein's ideas that teaching and learning are enhanced by mediating sharing.

Reflect on the following views that link to mediation of sharing:

Through others, we become ourselves.

—L. S. Vygotsky

Every creative act of ours in relation to other people—an act of love, of pity, of help, of peacemaking—not merely has a future but is eternal.

—Nicholas Berdyaev

Alone we can do so little; together we can do so much.

—Helen Keller

Consider

Consider the teaching and learning strategy of cooperative learning that was proposed by theorists Johnson and Johnson (1974) and others. The simple principle of this approach is that students learn better when they work together. Theorists believe that when learners work cooperatively they are more efficient, their understanding improves, and they feel more positive about their learning experience. Success is achieved because the competitive element of learning is replaced by group cohesion where students can both give and take to improve learning for all. Effective cooperative learning involves four key principles:

1. Positive interdependence (where everyone feels valued as part of the group)
2. Individual accountability (where each learner must contribute something)
3. Task and process evaluation (where the individual and group assess their work and their interaction)
4. Cooperative learning skills (where general skills such as clear communication and specific skills such as leader, note-taker, etc., are understood)

Learning with a peer or in groups, cooperatively, links well with Feuerstein's view of mediating sharing where learners work together to achieve a common goal.

If you have an apple and I have an apple and we exchange apples then you and I will still each have one apple. But if you have an idea and I have an idea and we exchange these ideas, then each of us will have two ideas.

—George Bernard Shaw

Learning is a social process that occurs through interpersonal interaction within a cooperative context. Individuals, working together, construct shared understandings and knowledge.

—David Johnson

Work Page ....

Think of your own understanding of learning. What other ideas, approaches, theories, or practices can you link with Feuerstein's concept of mediation of sharing?

_____

_____

_____

_____

_____

_____

_____

_____

_____

_____

_____

_____

_____

_____

_____

_____

_____

_____

Work Page ·

Often class projects are organized in pairs or groups. Unfortunately, the more dominant, forceful, conscientious members tend to take over at the exclusion of other members.

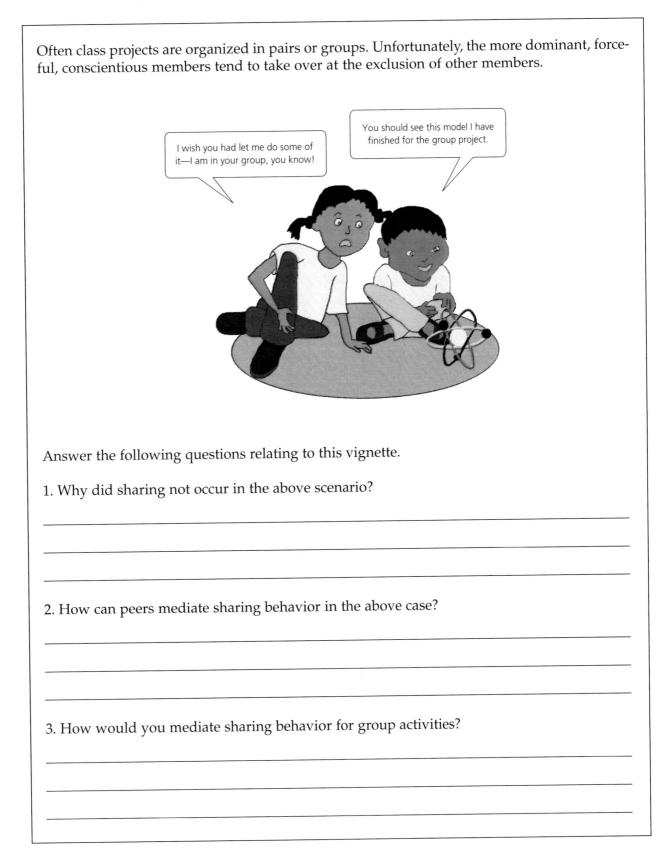

Answer the following questions relating to this vignette.

1. Why did sharing not occur in the above scenario?

_____

_____

_____

2. How can peers mediate sharing behavior in the above case?

_____

_____

_____

3. How would you mediate sharing behavior for group activities?

_____

_____

_____

Work Page ....

True or False

Write **T** below the true statements and **F** below the false statements.

1. The mother who puts away her children's toys is demonstrating sharing behavior. _____

2. A lack of mediation of sharing may result in an inability to form friendships. _____

Define

Define *sharing* in your own words.

_____

_____

_____

_____

Modify

Replace the following statement with one that would improve the mediation of sharing behavior.

"Finish your project by yourself."

_____

_____

_____

_____

Think About

Encouraging competition by posting class ranks and awarding prizes prepares students for life in a competitive society. Mediating sharing behavior, where competition is deemphasized, does not help students cope in today's individualistic world. What do you think?

_____

_____

_____

_____

Chapter **8**

Individuation

Individuation occurs when the mediator fosters a sense of uniqueness and difference within the learner. Mediation of individuation encourages autonomy and independence from others and celebrates the diversity of people.

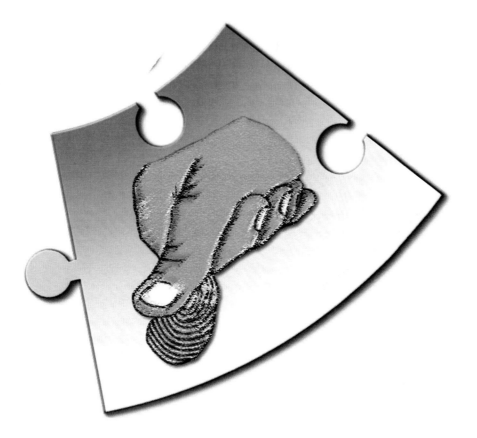

EXPLANATION

Individuation can be likened to a thumbprint, which is unique and different for each and every individual. Putting one's own independent and original mark on something would be like leaving one's thumbprint.

Mediation of individuation is the seventh piece of the Mediated Learning Experience puzzle. It involves fostering the development of the individual's autonomy and unique personality. The mediator acknowledges the differences among people due to past experiences, individual abilities, behavioral styles, motives, emotions, and other characteristics, and also encourages the learner to reach his or her own potential.

Parents, teachers, and caregivers who do not believe in the ability of a child to assume control and take responsibility for himself or herself will stifle the individuation and self-expression of that child. Such stifling of individuation could result in what Hopson and Scally (1981) refer to as "pinball living," in which individuals who are incapable of taking responsibility for their lives become like balls in a pinball machine which have no life of their own; they are set in motion by someone else and then bounce from one place to another without any clear direction, sometimes even making big scores, but then sinking into oblivion until someone sets them off again (Hopson & Scally, p. 52).

The opposite of pinball living is self-empowered living, which results from the mediation of individuation.

In the Classroom

The educators Belle Wallace and Harvey Adams (1993) describe two opposite teaching approaches. The first type, which they believe stifles individuation, is the inert curriculum. In this type of classroom, the teacher dominates.

- Teaching is content based and requires the rote recall of facts
- Students are passive and conforming and have an external locus of control (e.g., need extrinsic motivators)

The opposite approach to teaching, which enhances individuation, Wallace and Adams refer to as the enabling curriculum. In this type of classroom

- Learning is student oriented
- Teaching is process based and encourages autonomous learners
- Students take responsibility for their learning and have an internal locus of control (e.g., self-discipline)

Individuation in the classroom requires diversification of the teacher's approach and goals in order to meet students' individual differences in ability and temperament.

In the Home

By mediating individuation, the parent encourages a child to take control and responsibility for his or her daily activities. For example, by trusting the child to take care of his or her own pets, the parent promotes autonomy.

The parent who shows an interest in a child's hobbies will help to develop the unique personality of that child.

Remember

The various pieces of the Mediated Learning Experience puzzle work dynamically to balance and complement each other. The mediation of individuation, which promotes autonomy and independence, is balanced by the mediation of sharing, which fosters cooperation and interdependence (see Chapter 7).

It is an absolute perfection . . . to know how . . . to get the very most out of one's own individuality.

—Michel de Montaigne

APPLICATION

Examples

In the Classroom

The teacher accepts original responses.

"That's an interesting answer. Tell me how you came up with it."

Activities That Foster the Mediation of Individuation

- ☐ The teacher accepts divergent responses and encourages independent and original thinking.
- ☐ The teacher holds the students responsible for their behavior and assigns them responsible tasks.
- ☐ The teacher lets the students choose some of their classroom activities and encourages diversity in their use of free time.
- ☐ The teacher enhances the positive aspects of multiculturalism and ideological and religious differences.
- ☐ The teacher refrains from asking for total obedience and total identification with his or her values and beliefs.

In the Home

The parent praises individual talent.

"Mary, you're fantastic with animals. I'm glad you've decided to become a veterinarian."

- ☐ The parent respects the right of the child to be different—the "free-to-be-me" approach.
- ☐ The parent encourages the child to express some control over his or her behavior, thereby allowing the child to develop his or her own personality.
- ☐ The parent acknowledges and enjoys the unfolding of the child's interests and abilities.
- ☐ The family members respect one another's right to privacy.

In the Counseling/ Community Situation

The community worker models the acceptance of differences.

"Let's examine how our different values influence our perceptions of this problem."

- ☐ The community worker makes explicit the heterogeneous nature of the group and celebrates it as a valuable resource.
- ☐ The therapist encourages parents to develop boundaries among individuals in the family.
- ☐ The counselor helps the client to perceive herself or himself as worthy and competent, yet unique.
- ☐ The therapist bases interpretations on the client's perceptions of his or her world.
- ☐ The community worker encourages self-government by individuals in the group in areas pertaining to their expertise or interests.

MAKING LINKS

Mediation of individuation can be linked to ideas and approaches that have been developed by others who are involved in education. Consider some of the following ideas from educationists, psychologists, and theorists that support and complement Feuerstein's ideas that teaching and learning are enhanced by mediating individuation.

Reflect on the following views that link to mediation of individuation:

The principal goal of education is to create men who are capable of doing new things, not simply of repeating what other generations have done—men who are creative, inventive and discoverers.

—Jean Piaget

Each person's map of the world is as unique as their thumbprint. There are no two people alike . . . no two people who understand the same sentence the same way . . . So in dealing with people try not to fit them to your concept of what they should be.

—Milton Erickson

Consider

Consider the teaching approach called differentiated instruction. This method of teaching, proposed by educationalists such as Tomlinson (2001), is based on the belief that "no two students are alike." In this approach, all students are seen to have differing abilities and interests, so the "one size fits all" approach to teaching is ineffective. The key to differentiated instruction is flexibility—allowing for different learning goals, different ways of accessing information, and different ways of learning at varying levels of complexity depending on the specific individual learner. Contrasting a typical "traditional" style classroom with a "differentiated" classroom is an interesting way to illustrate this concept. In a traditional classroom, there is generally whole class instruction that is teacher initiated and directed. There is generally a single text and assignment option aimed at assessing "who got it." In contrast, in a differentiated classroom, student differences are assessed and used as a basis for multiple instructional approaches such as group work, peer tutoring, and individual problem-based learning using a variety of materials. Assessment is more formative and ongoing, and individual learning profiles are developed. In this approach, teaching and assessment are inseparable as the teacher adjusts the teaching according to the individual assessment of each different learner. This view of teaching seems to complement Feuerstein's view of mediating individuation where the uniqueness of each individual learner is acknowledged and celebrated.

You have your way. I have my way. As for the right way, the correct way, and the only way, it does not exist.

—Friedrich Nietzsche

I am not you and you are not me. Your hand is not mine and my hand is not yours. And you can't do things like me and I can't do things like you. And that's it.

—Tamar (4) to her grandmother,
as cited in Feuerstein, Rand, Rynders, 1988, p. 78

Work Page ....

Think of your own understanding of learning. What other ideas, approaches, theories, or practices can you link with Feuerstein's concept of mediation of individuation?

_____

_____

_____

_____

_____

_____

_____

_____

_____

_____

_____

_____

_____

_____

_____

_____

_____

_____

Work Page ·

Unfortunately, much of the literature we study at school has fixed interpretation set by authors and experts.

Answer the following questions relating to this vignette.

1. Think of an example you have experienced which links in to the above scenario.

_____

_____

_____

2. Comment on the teacher's mediation of individuation.

_____

_____

_____

3. Mediation of individuation involves allowing a child to take responsibility for decisions and become self-empowered. To what extent and in what way is Taiko responding in this regard?

_____

_____

_____

Work Page ·

True or False

Write **T** below the true statements and **F** below the false statements.

1. Acknowledging the differences among individuals is mediating individuation. _____

2. Unquestioning obedience to authority is compatible with individuation. _____

Define

Define *individuation* in your own words.

_____

_____

_____

_____

Modify

Replace the following statement with one that would improve the mediation of individuation.

"Dad will be so proud when you are old enough to carry on the family business."

_____

_____

_____

_____

Think About

Mediating individuation results in selfishness and egocentric behavior and could pave the way for greed and power-seeking behavior. Cooperation, along with democratic and collective values, are incompatible with individuation. What do you think?

_____

_____

_____

_____

Chapter 9

Goal Planning

M ediation of goal planning occurs when the mediator guides and directs the learner through the processes involved in setting, planning, and achieving goals by making the process explicit.

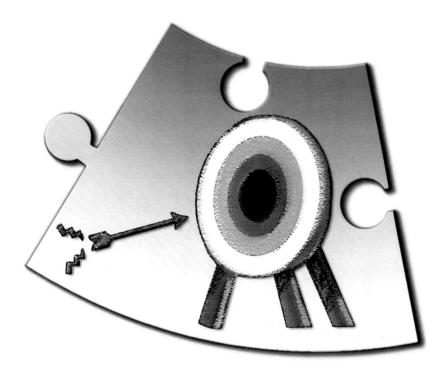

EXPLANATION

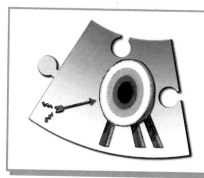

Goal planning can be likened to setting your sights on a target and developing a strategy to aim for and hit the bull's eye.

Mediation of goal planning is the eighth piece of the Mediated Learning Experience puzzle. It involves encouraging and guiding the learner to set goals and discussing explicit means for achieving them. Elaboration ofs process in goal-directed behavior is equally as important as accomplishing the task. The learner takes initiatives in setting, seeking, and reaching objectives.

Effective goals should be

- Conceivable—the learner should be able to conceptualize, understand, and identify the goal
- Believable—it is difficult to believe in a goal if the learner has never seen it achieved by someone else
- Achievable—be perceived by the student as
- Accomplishable—within her or his capabilities
- Modifiable—capable of being monitored and adapted
- Desirable—the learner must sincerely want to fulfill the goal, rather than feel obliged to
- Growth facilitating—not destructive to the learner, to others, or to society

Children can be impulsive; they have a strong desire for immediate gratification. This can manifest itself on both ends of the spectrum—in the overindulged child and in the deprived child.

The overindulged child whose requests are immediately satisfied never learns to delay gratification and engage in long-term goal planning. The deprived child, such as a homeless child, who has to live in the "here-and-now" in order to satisfy his or her basic needs for survival, does not have the opportunity to develop the skills for long-term planning.

When faced with a child in either of these scenarios, the counselor must help the child to develop the ability to delay gratification and feel more in control of achieving goals through understanding the processes involved. This will lead to greater self-confidence, empathy, autonomy, and more positive, resourceful, and independent learning.

Note

The five aspects of goal planning and achievement are

1. Setting goals that are realistic and appropriate to the situation

2. Planning how those goals can be achieved

3. Taking the steps to achieve the goals

4. Evaluating and reviewing the process of achieving the goals

5. Modifying and adjusting the goals as needed

Remember

Mediation of goal planning is inextricably linked to the other criteria of the Mediated Learning Experience puzzle, namely

- Competence—achieving goals results in a positive self-concept (see Chapter 5)
- Self-regulation and control of behavior—monitoring behavior facilitates reaching goals (see Chapter 6)
- Individuation—setting goals promotes autonomy and uniqueness (see Chapter 8)
- Challenge—the excitement of achieving a goal reinforces a sense of challenge (see Chapter 10)
- Self-change—awareness of reaching a goal develops an understanding of self-change (see Chapter 11)
- Optimistic alternative—planning goals that have a positive and desirable outcome (see Chapter 12)

It furthers one to have somewhere to go.

—The *I Ching* 28+32

APPLICATION

Examples

In the Classroom

The teacher assists in decision making.

"You need to clarify and set a strategy for achieving your long-term career goals through the right choice of subjects now."

In the Home

The caregiver elicits a strategy.

"Let's plan how we can raise $50 to donate to the Humane Society."

In the Counseling/ Community Situation

A community worker encourages reevaluation.

"At this phase of the project, let's review our progress and see if we need to redefine our goal."

Activities That Foster the Mediation of Goal Planning

☐ The teacher models goal-directed behavior by setting clear goals for each lesson and for learning in general.

☐ The teacher fosters the students' need to set realistic goals.

☐ The teacher encourages perseverance, patience, and diligence in the pursuit of goals.

☐ The teacher develops the students' ability to plan, review, and modify goals according to changing needs and circumstances.

☐ The teacher promotes in the students an autonomous attitude toward their futures.

☐ The teacher takes into account the students' interests and self-perceptions when helping them set goals.

☐ The parent elicits the help of the child in planning activities.

☐ The caregiver encourages the child to persevere with a task until the desired outcome is achieved.

☐ The father helps the child break down a long-term project into smaller parts and systematic stages.

☐ The parents help the child to reevaluate and set more appropriate and realistic goals when confronted with failure.

☐ The community worker elicits a plan of action from the group—a clarification of the goal, the ways of achieving it, and the possible outcomes.

☐ The community worker helps the individual modify and prioritize goals in order to solve the problem at hand.

☐ The therapist encourages the client to persevere and follow through with the project.

☐ The counselor rewards small advances toward a long-term goal.

MAKING LINKS

Mediation of goal planning can be linked to ideas and approaches that have been developed by others who are involved in education. Consider some of the following ideas from educationists, psychologists, and theorists that support and complement Feuerstein's ideas that teaching and learning are enhanced by mediating goal planning.

Reflect on the following views that link to mediation of goal planning:

Everything can be taken away from man but one thing—to choose one's attitude in a given set of circumstances, to choose one's own way.

—Viktor Frankl

To climb steep hills requires slow pace at first.

—William Shakespeare

If you don't know where you are going, any road will get you there.

—Lewis Carroll

Consider

There is a plethora of research in both academic and business domains on the concept of goal-directed behavior. Consider the work done by Hayes and his colleagues (1985) in which college students who were having serious problems with studying were selected. They were taught how to set specific study goals, which they made clear to the researchers. These students performed significantly better on tests covering the studied material than those students who worked on their own. Another study conducted by Morgan (1985) combined goal planning, self-recording, and self-evaluation. He taught these skills to his educational psychology students by setting specific short-term objectives for each study unit and monitored their progress toward the objectives. These students outperformed those who simply monitored study time.

The goal-setting phase is thus very important in self-management. This thought is echoed in the work of Feuerstein, which emphasizes the need to mediate goal-planning behavior to children.

If you plan on being anything less than you are capable of being, you will probably be unhappy all the days of your life.

What a man can be, he must be. This need we call self-actualization.

—Abraham Maslow

Work Page ....

Think of your own understanding of learning. What other ideas, approaches, theories, or practices can you link with Feuerstein's concept of mediation of goal planning?

_____

_____

_____

_____

_____

_____

_____

_____

_____

_____

_____

_____

_____

_____

_____

_____

_____

_____

Work Page ·

We often miss opportunities to encourage children to have goal-planning behavior. We tend to favor instant gratification and expediency in dealing with problems.

Dad, I really want a new skateboard now.

Sure, son, we'll go and buy one this weekend.

Answer the following questions relating to this vignette.

1. What are the short-term and the long-term goals that Pedro's father is mediating to Pedro?

_____

_____

_____

2. Effective goal planning occurs when goals are realistic and appropriate. How could Pedro's father mediate this to Pedro?

_____

_____

_____

3. Comment on ways that we could encourage children to satisfy their needs through goal-planning behavior.

_____

_____

_____

Work Page ·

True or False

Write **T** below the true statements and **F** below the false statements.

1. A poor conception of time interferes with effective goal planning. _____

2. A goal is not achieved if the plan is modified. _____

Define

Define *goal planning* in your own words.

_____

_____

_____

_____

Modify

Replace the following statement with one that would improve the mediation of goal planning.

"In looking at the results of your career assessment, I think you are best suited for a career in engineering."

_____

_____

_____

_____

Think About

Consistent planning for the future prevents students from truly experiencing the present. Mediating goal planning results in transmitting neuroses about time, deadlines, and the consequences of actions, all of which stifle spontaneity. What do you think?

_____

_____

_____

_____

Chapter 10

Challenge

Mediation of challenge occurs when the mediator instills in the learner a feeling of determination and enthusiasm to cope with novel and complex tasks. Identifying the steps involved in achieving success provides motivation for facing further challenges.

EXPLANATION

Mediation of challenge can be likened to exploring new and strange territories. Like climbing a mountain, it requires determination to persevere. The emotional peaks the explorer experiences are the excitement of success.

Mediation of challenge is the ninth piece of the Mediated Learning Experience puzzle. It involves evoking in the learner the motivation to attempt something new and the determination to persevere with something difficult. In a world that is constantly and rapidly changing, novelty and complexity become the norm, and mediating challenge helps prepare the learner to master these changes. It involves overcoming both a fear of the unknown and a resistance toward anything difficult or unusual.

Mediation of challenge can be achieved in a number of ways.

- The mediator can model an open and excited attitude when faced with new and difficult situations.
- The mediator can create opportunities for the learner to face novel and complex tasks.
- The mediator can encourage creativity, curiosity, and originality in confronting new tasks.
- The mediator can reward success and reflect the learner's feeling of satisfaction and excitement.
- The mediator can encourage sensible and appropriate risk taking in relation to different tasks and situations.

In the Classroom

An overemphasis on grades can have the negative effect of removing the intrinsic value of succeeding at a task. The result is that the student becomes motivated solely by external considerations. In addition, fear of failure inhibits attempts to take on new tasks or to try new and different approaches. The teacher can reduce such fears and mediate challenge by providing practice with unfamiliar tasks and breaking complex activities into smaller and more manageable sections. In addition, he or she can encourage risking initial failure when trying innovative approaches by placing less emphasis on the product and more on the process.

In the Home

We are all born with a natural desire for challenge. Toddlers struggle with manipulating a knife and a fork or with tying their shoes because they want to do these things by themselves. A parent who interferes and does the "difficult" tasks for the child is denying the child the practice needed to eventually succeed in mastering complex tasks.

Remember

The various criteria of the mediated learning experience puzzle are all related to each other. In this instance, a dynamic tension exists between the mediation of challenge and the mediation of meaning—in mediating meaning, conserving conventional values is emphasized (see Chapter 3); in mediating challenge, striving for something novel is emphasized.

Novelty is there to be learned and complexity is there to be mastered.

—Reuven Feuerstein

APPLICATION

Examples

In the Classroom

The teacher reduces anxiety toward a difficult problem.

"These are difficult examples. Let's see how many we can manage."

In the Home

The parent encourages.

"Try the big slide; you'll see it's a lot of fun."

In the Counseling/ Community Situation

The community worker makes explicit the process for success.

"This new and demanding project will require patience and initiative."

Activities That Foster the Mediation of Challenge

☐ The teacher makes available to students challenging, novel, and complex situations in accordance with their competence.

☐ The teacher encourages intellectual curiosity, originality, and creativity and presents unconventional tasks to students within a nonjudgmental climate.

☐ The teacher cites examples of people who have excelled in facing challenging, novel, and complex situations and in overcoming obstacles.

☐ The teacher makes the students aware of their growing ability to cope with novel and complex situations by focusing on the positive aspects of their work, even when the overall results are unsatisfactory.

☐ The parent stimulates the child's curiosity and invites him or her to explore new territory.

☐ The parents act as models for their children as they challenge themselves in new areas of growth.

☐ The caregiver shows excitement and anticipation when faced with a new and different situation, rather than protecting the child from the unknown.

☐ The parent provides a choice of activities to stimulate growth beyond the child's present level of development.

☐ The parent encourages the child to experience struggling with a difficult activity rather than doing it for him or her.

☐ The counselor develops the client's confidence to handle complex situations without fear by helping him or her to see the tasks as opportunities for growth.

☐ The therapist encourages the client to confront and eventually master situations previously avoided.

☐ The community worker models a positive feeling of anticipation in facing a new and changing environment.

☐ The therapist provides a nonjudgmental and supportive climate that facilitates experimentation.

MAKING LINKS

Mediation of challenge can be linked to ideas and approaches that have been developed by others who are involved in education. Consider some of the following ideas from educationists, psychologists, and theorists that support and complement Feuerstein's ideas that teaching and learning are enhanced by mediating challenge.

Reflect on the following views that link to mediation of challenge:

The ultimate measure of a man is not where he stands in moments of comfort and convenience, but where he stands in times of challenge and controversy.

—Martin Luther King, Jr.

Smooth seas do not make skilful sailors.

—African Proverb

Anything unattempted remains impossible.

—Anonymous

Our task, regarding creativity is to help children climb their own mountains, as high as possible.

—Loris Malaguzzi

The impossible is often the untried.

—Jim Goodwin

Consider

Current practice in special education has moved to including all children within the mainstream classroom. This practice of inclusion encompasses the philosophy of challenging people with learning difficulties. Since 1975, Public Law in the United States has ruled in favor of Least Restrictive Environment. Neverstreaming is a concept developed by Slavin (1991) to keep all students challenged to extend their learning experience levels. Providing challenging environments, both socially and academically, is preferable to the "dumbing down" syndrome, where the environment is adapted to just maintain the status quo. Including all students within the regular classroom challenges not only the learner but also the teacher and fellow classmates to support the learner to achieve. In Feuersteinian terms, inclusion challenges all involved with the learner to accommodate difference and help the learner overcome fears and barriers to learning in the regular classroom.

I won't teach her anything she already knows. I will teach her only things she doesn't know, and I will also teach her how to master them.

—Feuerstein, Rand, & Rynders, 1988, p. 82

Work Page ....

Think of your own understanding of learning. What other ideas, approaches, theories, or practices can you link with Feuerstein's concept of mediation of challenge?

_____

_____

_____

_____

_____

_____

_____

_____

_____

_____

_____

_____

_____

_____

_____

_____

_____

_____

Work Page ·····························

Often we miss opportunities because we perceive them to be out of our reach. We do not have the self-belief to attempt the challenge.

Answer the following questions relating to this vignette.

1. Does Sulamen mediate challenge?

_____

_____

_____

2. What does Mia's response tell us about her attitude to challenge? Why do you think she has this attitude?

_____

_____

_____

3. How could Sulamen respond in order to counter her feelings of insecurity and thus mediate challenge effectively?

_____

_____

_____

Work Page ....

True or False

Write **T** below the true statements and **F** below the false statements.

1. Mediating challenge contradicts the need to conserve the values and attitudes communicated to the learner through mediation of meaning. _____

2. Breaking a task down into simpler and familiar steps mediates challenge. _____

Define

Define *mediation of challenge* in your own words.

_____

_____

_____

_____

Modify

Replace the following statement with one that would improve the mediation of challenge.

"If you don't stick to what's tried-and-true, you will be disappointed."

_____

_____

_____

_____

Think About

Mediating challenge can encourage unnecessary exploration that might go beyond the child's capabilities; this is inadvisable. What do you think?

_____

_____

_____

_____

Chapter 11

Self-Change

M ediation for self-change occurs when the mediator encourages the learner to be aware of the dynamic potential for change and to recognize its importance and value.

EXPLANATION

Awareness of self-change is like plotting one's progress on a chart. The overall picture gives an indication of how much one has changed. The responsibility for the fluctuations in the graph, however, lies with the individual.

Mediation for self-change develops the learner's responsibility for continual personal change. This must occur if the learner is to become an independent and autonomous learner.

Feuerstein believes that human beings are endowed with a propensity for change. It is an inevitable process despite the fact that one may be neither aware of nor take full responsibility for it. In addition, some individuals resist change. For them, it is easier to remain in the "comfort zone," an area where their level of competence is not challenged.

Essentially, an awareness of self-change involves

- A recognition of self-change—that change comes from within oneself
- An expectation of growth—that levels of competence are always changing and improving
- A monitoring of change—mapping the changes that take place
- A welcome of and acceptance of change—that people are supposed to change

In the Classroom

The teacher who deemphasizes labels, who believes that ability levels are not static or permanent, and who encourages students to use a progress chart is communicating the value of being aware of self-change.

In the Home

Children love to hear parents and grandparents recite stories of when they were young. The family photo album, a "baby book," and wall growth charts are all items that sensitize children to their growth and change.

Remember

All the criteria of the Mediated Learning Experience puzzle are interlinked. Self-change is linked to

- Challenge—an awareness of self-change makes us less fearful of the unknown and enthusiastic about facing more complex tasks (see Chapter 10)
- Competence—an awareness of self-change prevents negatively labeling oneself as a failure. Failure with a task is not necessarily permanent. With experience and practice, failure changes to success. Success is not absolute but relative to previous performance (see Chapter 5)
- Goal planning—an awareness of self-change helps one to think about the future and anticipate and plan long- and short-term goals (see Chapter 9)

Change is the most stable characteristic of human beings.

—Reuven Feuerstein

APPLICATION

Examples

Activities That Foster the Mediation of Self-Change

In the Classroom

The teacher generates an awareness of self-change.

"Your handwriting has really improved; it's much more legible now."

☐ The teacher encourages self-evaluation of individual progress.

☐ The teacher deemphasizes labeling and its consequent self-fulfilling prophecy (e.g., the belief that IQ scores are meaningful).

☐ The teacher helps the students monitor self-change.

☐ The teacher helps the students understand that changing does not make one a different person.

☐ The teacher helps the students to become autonomous learners with internal criteria for evaluating progress.

☐ The teacher discourages comparison of results among students (e.g., class rankings).

In the Home

The parent points out the advantages of change.

"Now that you're more responsible, you can stay out later."

☐ The caregiver helps the child monitor his or her development (e.g., by plotting a growth chart).

☐ The parent also experiences change to accommodate changes that occur in the child.

☐ The parent shares positive perceptions of change occurring in the child.

☐ The caregiver makes explicit the benefits of maturation.

☐ The parent encourages the child to compare the progression of his or her report card throughout the school year.

In the Counseling/ Community Situation

The therapist rejects the static perception of the client.

"It's exciting to see your improvement. Let's record it on your progress chart."

☐ The counselor instills in the client a desire for self-development by demonstrating how to evaluate growth.

☐ The therapist mediates a sense of optimism in the family's ability to change dysfunctional patterns of interaction.

☐ The community worker assists the group in overcoming resistance to change within the community.

☐ The community worker focuses on the dynamic nature of both the group and its individual members in order to overcome a static and rigid interpretation of problems.

MAKING LINKS

Mediation of self-change can be linked to ideas and approaches that have been developed by others who are involved in education. Consider some of the following ideas from educationists, psychologists, and theorists that support and complement Feuerstein's ideas that teaching and learning are enhanced by mediating self-change.

Reflect on the following views that link to mediation of self-change:

When we are no longer able to change a situation—we are challenged to change ourselves.

—Viktor Frankl

Education does not make us educable. It is our awareness of being unfinished that makes us educable.

—Paulo Freire

The only person who is educated is the one who has learned how to learn . . . and change.

—Carl Rogers

I can't go back to yesterday—because I was a different person then.

—Lewis Carroll

Consider

Consider the research done by Rosenthal and Jacobson (1968), who wanted to see whether labeling a learner brought about change in the learner's behavior. In a now classic study called "Pygmalion in the Classroom," Rosenthal and Jacobson gave an IQ test to a class of students. They then selected at random, without any reference to the actual test scores, 20% of the class and told teachers that these students were expected to "bloom" in the coming year. They retested at the end of the next year and found that the students who they "predicted" would "bloom" had indeed improved in their IQ tests significantly more than the other students. Rosenthal and Jacobson concluded that labeling *does* matter and does bring about a change in the learner, as the teachers and learners start behaving in a way that is consistent with that label.

Generally, learners live *up or down* to the expectations put on them, so in mediating for self-change it is our moral responsibility as educators to mediate positive expectations. This notion of the self-fulfilling prophecy, and the evidence that learners reflect and monitor their own behavior in terms of these expectations, can be linked to Feuerstein's mediation of self-change and the importance of mediating a positive sense of self for learners to live up to.

. . . You see, really and truly, apart from the things anyone can pick up (the dressing and the proper way of speaking, and so on) the difference between a lady and a flower girl is not how she behaves, but how she's treated. I shall always be a flower girl to Professor Higgins, because he always treats me as a flower girl, and always will; but I know I can be a lady to you, because you always treat me as a lady, and always will.

—Eliza Doolittle in *Pygmalion* by George Bernard Shaw

Work Page ··

Think of your own understanding of learning. What other ideas, approaches, theories, or practices can you link with Feuerstein's concept of mediation of self-change?

_____

_____

_____

_____

_____

_____

_____

_____

_____

_____

_____

_____

_____

_____

_____

_____

_____

Work Page ·

In mediating for self-change, counselors encourage students to reflect on the positive outcomes of changing behavior.

Answer the following questions on the above vignette.

1. Self-change involves an awareness that change comes from within. Is there any indication that Hans is open to self-change?

_____

_____

_____

2. Does the counselor mediate self-change?

_____

_____

_____

3. How does Hans's self-reflection transfer into other areas of self-change and development?

_____

_____

_____

Work Page ....

True or False

Write **T** below the true statements and **F** below the false statements.

1. Labeling a child as weak or exceptional conflicts with the mediation of self-change. _____

2. Praising a child for an activity immediately after mastering it mediates self-change. _____

Define

Define *mediation of self-change* in your own words.

_____

_____

_____

_____

Modify

Replace the following statement with one that would improve the mediation of self-change.

"You don't have any artistic talent."

_____

_____

_____

_____

Think About

Accepting a child's low level of functioning is the humane approach in teaching. Mediating self-change can raise parents' and students' expectations unrealistically and unfairly. What do you think?

_____

_____

_____

_____

Chapter 12

Search for the Optimistic Alternative

Mediation of the search for an optimistic alternative is when the mediator works with the learner to choose an optimistic, rather than a pessimistic, approach to a situation. A pessimistic orientation results in accepting the status quo, or believing no good can be done. An optimistic alternative enables solutions to be found.

EXPLANATION

Imagine a glass has fifty percent of water in it. Is it half full or half empty? Both are right, but it depends on your outlook and your perspective. The pessimist will say "half empty" and see things negatively, while the optimist will say "half full" and will have a more positive perspective. The reality is that both are accurate; it is how we choose to view it that makes all the difference to our behavior. Mediating for the search for the optimistic alternative can be likened to perceiving the glass as half full and believing that life is full of the potential for positive change.

Mediation of the search for the optimistic alternative is the eleventh criterion of mediation and one of two criteria that Feuerstein added some time after presenting his initial ten criteria. This criterion links very closely with Feuerstein's view of "active modification." In outlining his Structural Cognitive Modifiability theory (see Part 1), Feuerstein identifies two orientations. The first is a "passive acceptance" approach, where the learner's deficits or difficulties are passively accepted and the environment has to accommodate these; here, the status quo, in terms of the learner's functioning, is maintained. The alternative approach is that of "active modification" where there is intensive intervention, or mediation, to actively modify learning so that the difficulties are overcome and significant changes occur in the mediatee's cognitive functioning. This active modification approach on the part of the mediator is aligned with the concept of mediating to the learner to search for an optimistic alternative. It parallels the belief in both the mediator and the learner that where there is a will to change and overcome difficulties, a way to do this will be found.

In the Classroom

This belief in the possibility of a positive outcome is essential to instill in learners in the classroom. Too often in current schooling practices, children with significant learning needs are segregated and put into "special classes" where their education is "dumbed down" to suit their current level of functioning. This instills in them the belief that there is no positive outcome, that the status quo is their only future. Often a curriculum is designed for a student based on the current level of functioning as determined by static psychometric tests such as intelligence tests. These intelligence tests measure where the learner is functioning at that particular moment in time, but too often they are used as predictors for the learner's future. Using this low score as a predictor of all future performance reduces the very possibility of change and reinforces the pessimistic, or passive acceptance, approach toward the learner. This stultifies in the learner the belief in an optimistic alternative and hence restricts the options generated to actively modify the learning and behavior. Intelligence tests cannot measure future performance, but often this is seen to be the case, with damaging consequences, when these tests continue to be seen to measure innate ability. As Gould (1981) points out, "We pass through this world but once. Few tragedies can be more extensive than the stunting of life, few injustices deeper than the denial of an opportunity to strive or even hope, by a limit imposed from without, but falsely identified as lying within" (p. 28).

In the Home

By mediating in the home the belief that there are many ways to view a situation, the parent will open up different opportunities for the family. For example, allowing different perspectives, opinions, and points of view to be expressed about a single event will mediate to the children in the family that there is never just one outcome. We need to help children view the glass as being half full. This will free them to be more positive about solving problems if they are empowered to dream of different optimistic solutions.

Remember

Mediation of the search for the optimistic alternative is clearly linked to the other criteria of mediation in the following ways:

- Competence—where an optimistic belief will contribute to the learner's positive self concept and sense of his or her ability to achieve
- Self-regulation and control of behavior—where an enabling optimistic approach will contribute to a sense of autonomy and responsibility
- Challenge—where the focus on finding positive solutions links to the sense of challenge
- Goal planning—where examining alternatives involves planning for positive courses of action

The pessimist sees difficulty in every opportunity. The optimist sees the opportunity in every difficulty.

—Winston Churchill

APPLICATION

Examples

In the Classroom

The teacher encourages students to feel free to think up a range of possible positive solutions.

"Let's first brainstorm all the wild and creative and inventive options we can think to solve pollution, and then we will evaluate them."

Activities That Foster Mediation of the Search for the Optimistic Alternative

☐ The English teacher explains how language is not neutral and the way we describe something can influence the way we represent it. Words both denote and connote—and our choice of words can influence the description and the meaning of something to be positive or negative (e.g., "terrorist" or "freedom fighter," "ignorant" or "learning difficulties").

☐ The teacher shows examples of ambiguous drawings to show how our perception can change if we choose to focus on the foreground or background. This perception influences our emotions and feelings as well as our ability to select the most effective course.

☐ The teacher encourages students to think positively about their future careers and set optimistic options to strive toward.

☐ The teacher shares examples of famous people who have found positive alternative outcomes to what could have been pessimistic futures (e.g., the life of Helen Keller).

In the Home

The parent encourages evaluative thinking about a problem.

"John, why don't we also list the positives as well as the negatives before you make a decision on what to do?"

☐ Family members look at setbacks in life as being starting points for future growth. Parents encourage multiple perspectives to be expressed about issues to enable children to see a variety of different options and alternatives to any given situation.

☐ Parents discuss family events to show how at any given point in time there was the possibility for a range of different outcomes and how there is a choice of following an optimistic route.

In the Counseling/ Community Situation

The therapist encourages an optimistic solution focused approach.

"When things are okay, how are they different? What makes it better? What can we work on to increase those times when it is better?"

☐ The counselor encourages the parents to explore a range of possibilities, options, and strategies in describing outcomes to a situation where they feel "stuck"' in their parenting.

☐ The therapist paints various scenarios of an event, describing it from different perspectives to enable the couple to see there are different ways to view their current situation, some more optimal than others.

☐ The community worker gets the group to do a "re-framing" exercise—where each member chooses something to describe in first a negative and then a positive way.

MAKING LINKS

Mediation of the search for the optimistic alternative can be linked to ideas and approaches that have been developed by others who are involved in education. Consider some of the following ideas from educationists, psychologists, and theorists that support and complement Feuerstein's ideas that teaching and learning are enhanced by mediating for an optimistic alternative.

Reflect on the following views that link to mediation of the search for an optimistic alternative:

When I look at the world I'm pessimistic, but when I look at people I am optimistic.

—Carl Rogers

If you only have a hammer, you tend to see every problem as a nail.

—Abraham Maslow

What we see depends mainly on what we look for.

—John Lubbock

An optimist expects his dreams to come true: a pessimist expects his nightmares to.

—Oscar Wilde

Consider

Consider the form of therapy called solution-focused therapy that was first introduced in the United States in the 1980's (Iverson, 2002). In this approach, there is a switch from a problem focus to a solution focus. Rather than delving into the problem to find the cause, the approach is centered on resources to find solutions. It's like the figure-ground drawing games—what aspect of the picture or situation do you choose to "see" and how does this perception influence your beliefs and then your actions? We perceive life through filters of our own beliefs. And we can choose for those filters to represent things in a way that there is no hope or choice or resolution, or in a way that provides challenge for a better future.

Solution-focused therapy, with its emphasis on finding solutions rather than focusing on problems, is compatible with Feuerstein's mediating a search for the optimistic alternative with the belief that where there is a will, there is a way to achieve a good outcome.

. . . one ship sails East, and another West,
By the self-same winds that blow,
'Tis the set of the sails and not the gales,
That tells the way we go.
Like the winds of the sea are the waves of time,
As we journey along through life,
'Tis the set of the soul, that determines the goal,
And not the calm or the strife.

—From *Winds of Fate* by Ella Wheeler Wilcox

Work Page ....

Think of your own understanding of learning. What other ideas, approaches, theories, or practices can you link with Feuerstein's concept of mediation of the search for the optimistic alternative?

_____

_____

_____

_____

_____

_____

_____

_____

_____

_____

_____

_____

_____

_____

_____

_____

_____

_____

Work Page ·

When we are emotionally embroiled in problems, or under stress, everything appears negative. The search for the optimistic alternative has to be mediated.

Answer the following questions on the above vignette.

1. How, if at all, does Nellie mediate the optimistic alternative to Garvan?

_____

_____

_____

2. What impact does the "half empty glass syndrome" have on Garvan?

_____

_____

3. How would you mediate the search for the optimistic alternative if you were Garvan's parent?

_____

_____

_____

Work Page ....

True or False

Write **T** below the true statements and **F** below the false statements.

1. Teachers who engage students in creative problem solving are mediating the search for the optimistic alternative. _____

2. The parent who focuses only on the punishment of negative behaviors is mediating the optimistic alternative. _____

Define

Define *mediation of the search for the optimistic alternative* in your own words.

_____

_____

_____

_____

Modify

Replace the following statement with one that would improve the mediation of the search for the optimistic alternative.

"You got half of your test wrong; you obviously don't have an aptitude for this."

_____

_____

_____

_____

Think About

Mediation of the search for the optimistic alternative implies that we always look for the bright side of life—the negatives are inconsequential and should rather be avoided. Is there an inherent danger in this? What do you think?

_____

_____

_____

_____

Chapter 13

Sense of Belonging

Mediation of a sense of belonging is when the mediator explains to the learner the value of being part of a larger family, group, community, and culture. Knowing about where and how we fit in, and having a common understanding of the way different cultures do things, promotes cognitive and socio-affective development.

EXPLANATION

We all have an instinctive need to know that we belong, to understand how we fit in, to feel that we are connected, supported, and linked. Understanding our past helps us live effectively in the present and plan for the future. Mediating a sense of belonging is like linking hands with the generation that came before us and the generation that comes after us. The cultural understanding we take with one hand from our parents, we pass on with the other hand to our children. We have a longing to be a part of our group, family, community, and culture—and we have a responsibility to mediate that sense of belonging.

Mediation of a sense of belonging is the final criterion of mediation, which Feuerstein introduced after presenting his initial ten criteria. This criterion links to the distinction that Feuerstein makes between cultural difference and cultural deprivation. Cultural difference relates to the idea that all cultures have different customs, rituals, beliefs, and practices that need to be mediated to the next generation of learners so that they are able to make sense of the world and develop the cognitive abilities to function effectively.

Cultural deprivation is when culture is not mediated, and the learner does not develop an understanding of how things work within their culture. When learners are deprived of their culture being mediated to them, they do not develop the necessary socio-cognitive skills to function effectively in their society. When culture is mediated from one generation to the next, and different cultures are celebrated, a sense of belonging is developed. Being deprived of the mediation of culture results in a lack of sense of belonging. So cultural difference involves understanding more about the cultural group to which one belongs, which might be different from another group. Cultural deprivation is being deprived of the mediation of that cultural understanding which results in a loss of a sense of belonging and impaired cognitive/affective development.

In the Classroom

The more we live in multicultural societies, the more important it is for schools to recognize and educate for that difference. Allowing learners to celebrate where they come from, and explain how they do things differently, aids both cognitive development as well as socio-affective qualities such as tolerance and empathy. There are many different groups to which a learner may belong and each of these groups has a particular "culture" too (e.g., a sports team, a music group, the debating club, the church choir). Mediating the mores, values, and practices of each of these, i.e., the "culture" of each these groups to learners, enables them to have a deeper sense of belonging to the group, thus improving their ability to contribute effectively.

In the Home

As family lifestyles become more fragmented, insular, and nuclear, we experience the danger of losing out on the benefits of generational interaction. Where lifestyles have meant a move away from extended family through separation, emigration, or relocation, there is the concern that the particular ways of functioning in a community or culture may be lost. Busy work schedules for families also can result in a lack of contact between the generations and hence less opportunity for the cultural rituals to be practiced and mediated from one generation to the next. There is then the risk of a learner experiencing anomie, or cultural alienation. The learner may experience a lack of understanding, a feeling of isolation, and a sense of not belonging anywhere. Families need to remember the value of passing on traditional understandings for the next generation.

Remember

Mediation of a sense of belonging is clearly linked to the other criteria of mediation in the following ways:

- Meaning—where understanding the cultural significance and purpose of a certain family practice increases the learner's sense of belonging
- Transcendence—where being able to see how everyday family activities are guided by underlying values, and where cultural principles will contribute to a sense of belonging
- Individuation—where understanding who we are and how we are different from others enables us at the same time to realize and appreciate where we belong

---

Whoever teaches his son teaches not alone his son but also his son's son, and so on to the end of generations.

—Hebrew Proverb

APPLICATION

Examples

In the Classroom

The teacher encourages students to reflect on traditions of the cultures to which they belong.

"For International Day, everyone can dress up in the costume of their culture and there'll be food and dances from the various groups."

In the Home

The parent tells stories of past generations to mediate a sense of belonging to the family.

"Well, your great-grandfather was a traveler who sailed to Africa and met your great-grandmother there and married and had nine children who...."

In the Counseling/ Community Situation

The counselor sets up the rights and responsibilities for belonging to the youth club.

"When you join the youth club, you can choose which sporting teams you want to belong to, but you have a commitment to your team to attend all practices and games and play by the rules."

Activities That Foster Mediation of Sense of Belonging

☐ The teacher develops a sense of belonging in the classroom by including all learners—especially those who have different and diverse learning needs.

☐ The teacher explores the roles and responsibilities that learners have in belonging to different groups—be they sporting clubs or musical groups or social clubs.

☐ The teacher collaborates and consults with people from the various communities and groups to which students belong to get a broader understanding of the various influences outside of the classroom that impact the students' learning.

☐ The teacher arranges "Cultural Awareness" days where students can dress and eat and celebrate in ways associated with their culture and traditions.

☐ Family members demonstrate a responsibility to support each other and develop a sense of interconnectedness between generations.

☐ Parents explain the religious or social significance of the different cultural practices of the family.

☐ Parents encourage their children to join sporting clubs and musical groups and to understand the values and rules of belonging to these groups.

☐ Families explore the roots of their language or religion or culture and compare these with other groups to foster understanding and empathy.

☐ The counselor encourages communities to work together to share responsibilities of making the environment to which they belong a better place.

☐ The therapist encourages clients to explore their roots to overcome a sense of isolation and anomie and develop a feeling of belonging.

☐ The social worker sets up youth clubs for street children and tries to instill a sense of responsibility and worth in belonging to these clubs.

MAKING LINKS

Mediation of a sense of belonging can be linked to ideas and approaches that have been developed by others who are involved in education. Consider some of the following ideas from educationists, psychologists, and theorists that support and complement Feuerstein's ideas that teaching and learning are enhanced by mediating for a sense of belonging.

Reflect on the following views that link to mediation of the search for a sense of belonging:

Learning and thinking are always situated in a cultural setting and always dependent upon the utilization of cultural resources.

—Jerome Bruner

I am a part of all that I have met.

—Alfred Tennyson

One generation plants the trees; another gets the shade.

—Chinese Proverb

It takes a village to raise a child.

—African Proverb

Consider

Consider the work of the psychologist Bronfenbrenner (1917–2005) whose ecological systems theory links to Feuerstein's sense of belonging. Bronfenbrenner proposed that a learner does not develop in isolation but in the context of the layers of family, community, and society. The layers that Bronfenbrenner outlined as impacting a learner's development include

- The microsystem—which is the innermost level closest to the learner and includes immediate environments such as the family, classroom, neighborhood, etc.
- The mesosystem—which involves the interconnection between immediate environments such as the interaction between the child's teacher and his parents, between his church and his neighborhood
- The exosystem—which is the social setting and defines the larger community influences on the child, like parental workplace
- The macrosystem—which is the outermost layer comprised of cultural values, customs, and laws

Each level contains roles, norms, and rules that shape the development of the individual. No leaner is an island—but exists through interacting with and through the various levels of family and society. Ecological theory, with its emphasis on acknowledging that every child belongs within a set of systems that extends outward from the family to community to culture, is compatible with Feuerstein's mediation of a sense of belonging.

> *How can we judge the worth of society? If the children and youth of a nation are afforded the opportunity to develop their capacities to the fullest, if they are given the knowledge to understand the world and the wisdom to change it, then the prospects for the future are bright.*
>
> —Urie Bronfenbrenner

Work Page ·····················

Think of your own understanding of learning. What other ideas, approaches, theories, or practices can you link with Feuerstein's concept of mediation of a sense of belonging?

_____

_____

_____

_____

_____

_____

_____

_____

_____

_____

_____

_____

_____

_____

_____

_____

_____

_____

Work Page ....

A key to understanding who we are is to investigate our roots and how they impact on our place in today's society. Teachers may cover this academically in history lessons, but there is a need to mediate a sense of belonging in all domains of a child's life.

Speech bubble 1: Out study of Chinese ancestry helps us appreciate the difficulties our families experienced in the past.

Speech bubble 2: Wow! My great grandfather fought in that war!

Answer the following questions on the above vignette.

1. How, if at all, does the teacher mediate a sense of belonging to Chang?

_____

_____

_____

2. What impact does this approach have on Chang that could be carried through to the future?

_____

_____

_____

3. How would you mediate a sense of belonging in your areas of specialization?

_____

_____

_____

Work Page ....

True or False

Write **T** below the true statements and **F** below the false statements.

1. The mother who shares family photos of her childhood with her son is mediating a sense of belonging. _____

2. The counselor who encourages the child to focus entirely on his or her own needs is mediating a sense of belonging. _____

Define

Define *mediation of a sense of belonging* in your own words.

_____

_____

_____

_____

Modify

Replace the following statement with one that would improve the mediation of sense of belonging.

"Your past is not important—it is where you are now that should be your focus."

_____

_____

_____

_____

Think About

Some therapies purposely avoid talking through early life family experiences or relationships that may be hurtful. They concentrate on modifying current behaviors and cognitions within the individual. Is this contradictory to the mediation of a sense of belonging?

_____

_____

_____

_____

PART III

Metacognition

Cognitive Functions and Dysfunctions

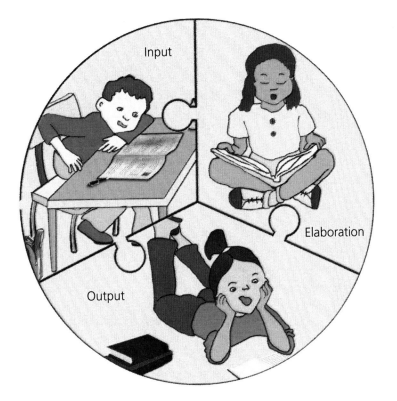

- What is cognition?

- What are the prerequisites of thinking?

- What does it mean to think about thinking, i.e., to engage in metacognition?

- How can parents and teachers help children learn how to learn?

Part III attempts to answer these questions by discussing Feuerstein's list of cognitive functions and dysfunctions.

This part is devoted to an elaboration of the cognitive functions/dysfunctions as identified by Reuven Feuerstein. It is not meant as a substitute for Feuerstein's own program of Instrumental Enrichment, which remains one of the best researched, most promising, and well-developed vehicles for teacher-student mediation and the development of cognitive functions.

It is recognized that many of the cognitive functions presented in this part may already be addressed by teachers, who may use some of the strategies presented here and/or their own. This part is presented to supplement the teacher's repertoire of strategies and his or her understanding of cognitive functions. Most important, the focus on cognitive functions and strategies for their enhancement is meant to bring these points to the attention of teachers, so that they can increase their awareness of, and thinking about, the processes and purposes of education and the most effective strategies for developing these processes and achieving their goals.

Furthermore, the analysis and undertaking of cognitive functioning in terms of underlying processes is seen as a more effective alternative to the traditional forms of psychometric assessment, which emphasize the quantification of children's abilities, offer a global approach to their measurement, and provide little link between assessment and intervention. Thus, this part is seen as providing the teacher with a tool to constructively assess and intervene in areas of difficulty.

At the same time, this part is relevant to students across the spectrum of ability, in that cognitive functions can always be enhanced. Moreover, a higher achieving student is not necessarily one who has developed those cognitive functions needed for autonomous learning in later life. Again, cognitive ability is relative, and there will be variations both within individuals (often marked) and across individuals in the degree of competence in any given function. There are also those for whom particular cognitive dysfunctions may be extremely difficult to remediate. In such cases, it is important to adopt a flexible approach and to find compensatory cognitive functions by which the student can achieve the same goals.

Finally, cognitive functions cannot be seen out of their cultural, developmental, situational, and emotional contexts. For example, what is considered necessary and/or desirable in one culture may be seen as irrelevant in another; what may be regarded as a deficiency at one age will be considered as developmentally appropriate at another; a student may exercise a cognitive function fully in one situation but, for motivational or emotional reasons, negate it in another. The issue may not relate to the student's cognitive functions at all, but may pertain to the characteristics/demands of the environment.

Thus, this part's cognitive functions and strategies are not presented in a prescriptive or diagnostic manner. They are meant as a guide to the goals and methods that teachers may adopt in enhancing cognitive functioning.

The list of cognitive functions is helpful in identifying and understanding the reasons for an individual's failure or poor performance on a task. Once the deficient functions have been identified, the individual may be helped by correcting and redeveloping these cognitive functions through appropriate and sufficient mediation. Thus, Feuerstein's list of cognitive functions, which is the core of his model of thinking, serves as a very useful assessment and teaching tool.

AIM OF COGNITION

The aim of this part is to explain and operationalize the cognitive functions and dysfunctions. It provides

- A detailed discussion of each cognitive function
- Practical examples of the cognitive dysfunctions
- Strategies for remediating the dysfunction in terms of MLE

We believe that Feuerstein's list of the cognitive functions, which is the prerequisite of cognition, is a valuable tool for

- Diagnosing errors in thinking
- Remediating dysfunction
- Enriching the cognitive function

This list can be used to help students become more autonomous and independent learners through being aware of, and understanding, their own thinking and behavior, i.e., exercising metacognition, or thinking about their own thinking.

COGNITIVE FUNCTIONS AND DYSFUNCTIONS: INPUT, ELABORATION, AND OUTPUT

All too often, a child's failure to perform a given operation, whether in the classroom or test situation, is attributed either to a lack of knowledge of the principles involved in the operation or, even worse, to a low intelligence that precludes his understanding of the principles. What is overlooked is that the deficiency may reside not in the operational level or in the specific content of the child's thought processes but in the underlying functions upon which successful performance of cognitive operations depends.

—Feuerstein, 1980, p. 71

Feuerstein has categorized the cognitive functions according to the three major phases of the mental act—namely input, elaboration, and output. Although artificially separated into three phases, they don't necessarily occur separately in life. However, the subdivision is useful to analyze and describe thinking as well as determine what factors might negatively affect thinking. This model can be used by teachers and parents to better understand and help the child who is experiencing difficulties with a particular task.

For example, if a child fails in the task of classification, it is not enough to comment on the child's poor intelligence or inability to classify—but rather, the underlying causes of the difficulty, which can be found in one of the three phases of thinking, should be sought. The inability to classify, for instance, may be due to underlying functions such as imprecise data gathering at the input phase, an inability to compare the items at the elaboration phase, or poor communication skills at the output phase.

A detailed analysis of a student's cognitive functions requires an in-depth understanding of the three phases of the mental act:

Input Phase: Taking in Information (Reception)

This is the phase in which information or data are gathered in order to solve a task. For example, it may involve efficient and accurate perception, adequate listening skills, solid understanding of the language and of the concepts of time, space, and quantity, as well as the ability to collect and examine many sources of information at one time.

Elaboration Phase: Working on the Problem (Processing)

This is the phase where the information or data are processed. Our minds work on the information we have gathered. For example, it may involve defining the task, comparing and integrating relevant sources of information, planning, hypothesizing, working through problems logically, and so on. This is the most important and central phase.

Output Phase: Communicating a Response (Expression)

This is the phase where the information or data are communicated or presented. Responses or answers to a problem are given. It involves accurate, appropriate, and efficient communication skills.

Chapter **14**

Input

I f one were to overhear some or all of these comments about a student's thinking, it is likely that the student is experiencing difficulty at the input phase of the thinking process.

- "Don't just guess, examine it in detail."
- "Slow down, take your time."
- "Are you lost?"
- "You must learn to look before you leap."
- "You've left out five important details."
- "Did you understand the story we read?"
- "What were the instructions?"
- "Let's figure out what stayed the same and what changed."
- "You need to work out a study timetable."
- "It's the same picture, only seen from a different angle."
- "Late again?"
- "Which is your right hand?"
- "You'll need to consider different points of view."
- "Your essay is off the topic."
- "Look carefully now."
- "These are just careless and silly mistakes."

INPUT PHASE

The "input," "elaboration," and "output" topography of an intellectual act has an obvious analogy with computer systems, and Feuerstein admits that, despite its comparative sophistication, it is still an over-mechanical analysis of the way children think. However, it has allowed Feuerstein to progress from general analysis and description of the causes of inadequate intellectual functioning in children to a system of diagnosis which can be picked up and

used by teachers, parents, and other professionals with a limited amount of training. (Sharron, 1987, p. 58)

Feuerstein has grouped the processes underlying thinking, or the cognitive functions, into three phases—input, elaboration, and output.

1. At the input phase, information is gathered in order to undertake a task or solve a problem.

2. At the elaboration phase, information is processed.

3. At the output phase, the response is communicated.

At the input phase, stimuli around us are absorbed by our senses of sight, smell, taste, touch, and hearing. Difficulties experienced at this stage will affect how the task is tackled at the elaboration phase and how the product is expressed or presented at the output phase. For example, a student with difficulties at the input phase may rush blindly into a task without taking the time to examine all the necessary information. This student may often be late, get lost, misunderstand verbal instructions, or have difficulty following a story. Such a student may also make careless mistakes, leave out important details, or fail to see the similarities among stimuli.

This chapter deals with problems at the input phase of thinking. A detailed explanation of how to identify each dysfunction is provided and suggestions are made for correcting it using Feuerstein's criteria of mediation.

Use this table to identify each child's cognitive dysfunction in the classroom illustration on the opposite page.

Input	
Functions	**Dysfunctions**
Perception	
Clear	Blurred and Sweeping
Exploration of a Learning Situation	
Systematic	Impulsive
Receptive Verbal Tools and Concepts	
Precise and Accurate	Impaired
Understanding of Spatial Concepts	
Well Developed	Impaired
Understanding of Temporal Concepts	
Well Developed	Lack of or Impaired
Ability to Conserve Constancies	
Well Developed	Impaired
Data Gathering	
Precise and Accurate	Impaired
Capacity to Consider More Than One Source of Information	
Well Developed	Impaired

PERCEPTION

Description

What characterizes blurred perception is a poverty of details or their lack of clarity . . . and an incompleteness of the data necessary for proper distinction and description. (Feuerstein, 1980, p. 76)

The student's sweeping perception causes a lack of understanding.

Clear Perception

Clear perception refers to the ability to

- Focus attention long enough to perceive relevant details
- Clearly differentiate between essential or relevant details and extraneous or irrelevant details
- Define and describe the attributes of an object or problem
- Use past experience to analyze new information meaningfully
- Perceive all aspects of a problem holistically, that is, to integrate all parts
- Invest appropriate attention and time to detail depending on the novelty and complexity of the task

Blurred and Sweeping Perception

Blurred and sweeping perception could be identified by the following:

- Poor attention to form, shape, size, and space
- Poor discrimination of letters that look alike (e.g., confuses e and c)
- Poor discrimination of letters that sound alike (e.g., confuses i and e)
- An inability to select relevant details (e.g., focuses on background noise [a car passing] rather than the teacher's voice or can't focus on a specific visual item in a picture)

Various Occurrences

The manner in which things are perceived occurs at the input phase, in which the student receives information from the outside world. He or she integrates this information with existing knowledge at the elaboration phase in order to solve problems. The response is communicated at the output phase. Blurred or undifferentiated perception will result in incomplete and inaccurate data gathering that will interfere with cognitive processing and communication.

Example

A student with blurred and sweeping perception may guess at words based on general configurations when reading (e.g., reads petal instead of pedal [inaccurate perception]; reads a story problem too rapidly and misses an essential numerical detail that is necessary to solve the problem [incomplete perception]).

STRATEGIES

| Examples | Strategies to Correct Blurred and Sweeping Perception |

Intentionality and Reciprocity

The teacher gives a strategy for focusing attention.

"Read slowly and carefully so you don't miss any details."

☐ Facilitate letter recognition by linking the letter with a known object (e.g., link the letter S with the image of a snake).

☐ Use color, tracing, or magnification to help students visually perceive differences between letters in words (e.g., "pat" and "put").

☐ Reinforce the need to invest sufficient time in accurate data gathering by encouraging slow and systematic attention to the task.

Self-Regulation and Control of Behavior

The teacher encourages the student's self-regulation.

"Before answering, make sure you have considered all the information."

☐ Encourage students to describe in detail the information they have received.

☐ Allow students to stop periodically and re-describe the information in their own words.

☐ Reinforce the importance of self-monitoring (e.g., by slowing down, working accurately, and self-checking).

Competence

The teacher praises responses.

"Excellent, Sally! Tell us how you know that."

☐ Boost students' confidence to work independently in interpreting incoming information rather than relying exclusively on the teacher's input.

☐ Reward students for sharing strategies of successful data gathering.

☐ Reinforce a particular skill using more than one modality (e.g., read—repeat—write).

☐ Use contextual clues to aid accurate perception (e.g., using the sentence or passage to help decode the meaning of a word).

EXPLORATION OF A LEARNING SITUATION

Description

When presented with a number of cues that must be scanned, the individual's approach is so disorganized that he is unable to select those cues whose specific attributes make them relevant for a proper solution. (Feuerstein, 1980, p. 77)

> I know, I know the answer. You don't have to finish the question.

The student responds before the instructions are complete.

Systematic Exploration of a Learning Situation

Systematic exploration of a learning situation refers to the ability to

- Approach a task in a goal-oriented way
- Take time to gather and assess all the information needed to define a problem
- Think through a task in an ordered and systematic way
- Control speed and precision when solving a problem

Impulsive Exploration of a Learning Situation

The student who experiences difficulties with this cognitive function could manifest impulsivity in one of three ways. He or she will

- Rush into tasks too quickly in a haphazard and disorganized way, without appropriate attention to what is required, or without adopting a methodical approach
- Have poor investigational strategies, and will not see the need to gather and integrate all the information necessary to think through a problem
- Lack self-control and have difficulty adjusting the speed, accuracy, and precision needed for a particular task

Various Occurrences

Poor exploration of a learning situation will affect all three phases of thinking. In the input phase, it will manifest itself in a disorganized approach to a problem. In the elaboration phase, it will result in an inability to think through the problem systematically. In the output phase, it will be seen as a rushed and premature response.

Example

Impulsivity could manifest itself in the student blurting out answers before the teacher has finished giving instructions. He or she will engage in "trial-and-error" responses and not take the time to define the problem or look at all the information necessary to solve it. Although the student may consider all the information necessary to solve the problem, he or she will fail to integrate all the variables. For example, in piecing together a jigsaw puzzle, he or she may not consider color, shape, and size simultaneously.

STRATEGIES

Examples	Strategies to Correct Impulsivity

Intentionality and Reciprocity

The teacher slows the pace to ensure attention.

"Let's go slower and focus on one thing at a time."

☐ Structure the environment (e.g., reduce the quantity of stimuli in order to prevent the students from shifting between one task and another).

☐ Vary the students' exposure to the stimuli (e.g., introduce at a slower speed for a longer time).

☐ Allow students to use more than one modality in responding to a stimulus (e.g., oral and written responses).

☐ Repeat the instructions.

☐ Give students a plan or a model (specify the steps) to apply to the task.

Self-Regulation and Control of Behavior

The teacher encourages self-control.

"Wait a minute; let us think!"

☐ Delay the students' response (e.g., tell the students to think answers through before responding).

☐ Model problem solving by talking through the solution to problems.

☐ Encourage turn-taking to inhibit hasty responses.

☐ Allow students to explain the task in their own words.

Optimistic Alternative

The teacher calls for consideration of another alternative.

"Let's look at a better way to solve this problem."

☐ Give students immediate feedback or insight by providing them with other alternatives for their responses.

☐ Demonstrate the importance of gathering information before deciding what is the best alternative.

☐ Allow students to reflect and analyze their courses of action before choosing the one that has the greatest benefits.

☐ Demonstrate the value of taking a positive view before starting a challenging task.

RECEPTIVE VERBAL TOOLS AND CONCEPTS

Description

At the input phase, the absence of a verbal code . . . reduces the quantity and quality of gathered information. (Feuerstein et al., 1986, 3.7)

What is a triangle?

The student has difficulty understanding terms.

Precise and Accurate Receptive Verbal Tools

Precise and accurate receptive verbal tools refers to the ability to

- Understand concepts and related words in order to interpret incoming information
- Use language as a tool to receive information
- Use language as a system for reasoning and communication in social interactions
- Listen to and interpret (process) the language, which requires a knowledge of vocabulary, word, and sentence structure (grammar); meaning (semantics); and social and cultural contexts (pragmatics)

Impaired Receptive Verbal Tools

The student who has impaired receptive verbal tools and concepts may

- Listen to and interpret spoken language inaccurately even though his or her hearing is normal
- Misinterpret instructions and questions
- Have poor comprehension skills that will hamper the interpretation of incoming language

---

Various Occurrences

The absence of specific verbal tools to describe an object or concept will affect efficiency of data collection at the input phase. At the elaboration phase, lack of understanding of concepts such as "opposite," "similar," "different," etc., may impair the ability to think about and solve more complex abstract tasks. At the output phase, inadequate verbal expression impairs communication of insights, ideas, answers, and solutions.

Example

If the student does not understand the vocabulary used in the classroom, he or she will be unable to interpret information. If the student cannot label shapes (e.g., a square versus a triangle), classifying them will be difficult.

STRATEGIES

Examples	Strategies to Correct Impaired Verbal Skills
Competence	
The teacher adapts the task to the students' level of language competence. *"Let's rephrase this in a simpler and shorter way."*	☐ Determine the students' competence in the language of instruction and accommodate for their native language and/or English as a second language. ☐ Use language at a slightly higher level than that of the students in order to promote language development. ☐ Rephrase the language in a different way. ☐ Reduce the length and complexity of material (i.e., make it shorter and simpler). ☐ Provide concrete tools (e.g., illustrations, charts, drama, sequence cards, films, maps, graphs) to explain, reinforce, and elaborate verbal information.
Transcendence	
The teacher reinforces concepts using examples from the students' environment. *"Name five things in your bedroom that are bigger than your bed."*	☐ Provide the students with specific and accurate labels for a concept and model usage of these labels (i.e., "to name it is to know it"). ☐ Relate concepts to the students' everyday experiences. ☐ Encourage active discussion during presentation of information or material. ☐ Relate new words to students' existing vocabulary and encourage them to think about the meaning of words in a variety of contexts.
Meaning	
The teacher encourages meaningful use of language. *"Which witch is which?"*	☐ Make sure that information is age and culture appropriate and presented in a meaningful context. ☐ Develop "active listening" skills (i.e., listening for meaning). ☐ Develop language comprehension skills (e.g., categories, analogies, and ambiguities).

UNDERSTANDING OF SPATIAL CONCEPTS

Description

Both spatial and temporal concepts are needed to define our perceptions. The uniqueness of a [percept] is provided by inserting the object or event into a matrix of time and space. (Feuerstein et al., 1986, p. 83)

The student has difficulty explaining the way and points.

Well-Developed Understanding of Spatial Concepts

A well-developed understanding of spatial concepts refers to the ability to

- Understand how objects or people are physically positioned in space
- Accurately locate oneself in relation to others or objects (i.e., to formulate a personal reference system)
- Assess the relationships among objects or people
- Use labels that describe positions in space (e.g., left and right)

Impaired Understanding of Spatial Concepts

The student who has an impaired understanding of spatial concepts may

- Lack labels for adequately describing positions and relationships among objects (e.g., in front of, on top of, out, in)
- Not have an established personal spatial reference system (i.e., left and right)
- Experience difficulty in accepting the relativity of personal space (e.g., my left may be your right)
- Lack the ability to plan the use of space efficiently and appropriately
- Need to physically show and point rather than describe a set of directions
- Have difficulty coordinating body parts in space
- Have difficulty locating him- or herself mentally in space

Various Occurrences

At the input phase, spatial orientation helps an individual to accurately perceive and locate the relationship between objects and people. This permits the manipulation of spatial relationships at the elaboration phase. At the output phase, these relationships are communicated in a way that is universally understood.

Example

A student who has an impaired understanding of spatial concepts would prefer to point or physically lead someone to a specific location rather than explain how to get there.

STRATEGIES

Examples

Strategies to Correct an Impaired Understanding of Spatial Concepts

Intentionality and Reciprocity

The teacher provides an opportunity to experience space.

"Simple Simon says: 'Put your hands on your head, jump right. . . .'"

☐ Actively involve students in games that encourage the use of spatial concepts and language, such as
   – Verbal instructions for finding a hidden snack
   – Reading a treasure hunt map
   – Charting a yacht's course
   – Plotting a route through the Himalayas
☐ Use different methods to describe routes and locations (e.g., mapping, charting, and plotting).

Transcendence

The teacher expands ideas.

"Which political parties are to the right of center and which are to the left?"

☐ Compare the use of a personal reference system—left and right—to a stable system—north and south.
☐ Extend the understanding of how space and shape are related (e.g., in three-dimensional objects, geometry, perspective).
☐ Challenge the students to explore concepts such as infinity, negative numbers, the universe, and relativity.
☐ Bridge from the literal/physical use of space to the figurative (e.g., from idioms such as "moving up" to understanding what politically "left" and "right" means, to analyzing different "perspectives" on various topics).
☐ Encourage the development of empathy and the ability to see things through another's eyes.

Self-Regulation and Control of Behavior

The teacher encourages the student to rely on his or her own resources.

"Draw your own map of how to get to the grocery store."

☐ Boost students' confidence to work independently in interpreting incoming information, rather than relying exclusively on the teacher's input.
☐ Provide a concrete and personalized way of differentiating right from left (e.g., when asked to make a fist, an individual will generally do it with his or her dominant hand, that is, a right-handed person will clench his or her right hand).
☐ Give the students the responsibility of guiding and directing an adult to a local shop, their school, etc. (e.g., physically pointing, giving verbal directions, or drawing maps).

UNDERSTANDING OF TEMPORAL CONCEPTS

Description

Time is an abstract element and requires representational relational thinking . . . and is characterized by a need for ordering, summating, comparing, and sequencing, all of which must be produced initially by a volitional act on the part of the individual. (Feuerstein, 1980, p. 84)

The student reveals his confusion with time.

Well-Developed Understanding of Temporal Concepts

A well-developed understanding of temporal concepts refers to the ability to

- Understand the sequence and order of events (e.g., recalling a series of events in the correct chronological order)
- Understand how units of time are organized and summated (e.g., hours, days, weeks, months, and years)
- Make spontaneous comparisons between time concepts in order to gain meaning (e.g., "before" versus "after")
- Understand how the past has influenced the present and how actions in the present will have consequences for the future (i.e., cause and effect)
- Make use of past experiences or future anticipation in order to control behavior and organize time effectively

Lack of or Impaired Understanding of Temporal Concepts

The student who experiences a lack of or an impaired understanding of temporal concepts may

- Not understand or use timetables, calendar, or planner
- Not adhere to schedules (e.g., may be ready too early or too late)
- Perceive events out of context (e.g., might not be able to make cause-and-effect connections)
- Not understand outcomes of actions or events, and thus manifest problematic behavior
- Not be able to delay gratification and will expect immediate rewards (or punishment) for actions
- Feel confused because he or she is disoriented in time
- Not exhibit systematic exploratory behavior (e.g., retrace steps in order to find a lost article)

Various Occurrences

The concept of time is abstract and requires an understanding of the sequence of events. Therefore, a limited understanding of time concepts at the input phase will result in poor planning and organization of information at the elaboration phase. At the output phase, students will manifest an inability to spontaneously structure their daily activities.

Example

A young student might not understand that "today" becomes "yesterday" and that "tomorrow" becomes "today." This can result in the frustration of feeling that "tomorrow never comes."

STRATEGIES

Examples

Strategies to Correct an Impaired Understanding of Temporal Concepts

Meaning

The teacher helps the students to become conscious of time.

"You can't make up for lost time."

☐ Promote an understanding of the concept of time and units of time, such as day/night; morning/afternoon; before/after; days/weeks; and months/years (e.g., monitor the hours of light or dark, or the changes in seasons).

☐ Allow students to practice understanding the vocabulary of time, such as first/last; early/late (e.g., study story sequences).

☐ Help students to discover the value of ordering and sequencing information (e.g., use a history timetable).

Self-Regulation and Control of Behavior

The teacher provides an example of cause and effect.

"You missed the field trip because you were late for the bus."

☐ Help students to manage time effectively (e.g., year planners, calendars, timetables, homework diaries).

☐ Discuss cause-and-effect relationships in order to demonstrate the consequences of actions.

☐ Encourage students to plan activities and achieve tasks within specific time limits.

☐ Encourage students to attack problems using a controlled and systematic step-by-step method.

Sense of Belonging

The teacher clarifies for the student.

"Your father's father is your grandfather and he was born in 1910."

☐ Explore ways in which an understanding of time is valuable in establishing the student's place relative to the rest of the family.

☐ Discuss ways in which time is conceived differently in various cultures to which we belong (e.g., a nomad boy roaming the desert versus a city boy catching public transport).

☐ Show how time and timetables impact our family and social behaviors.

☐ Develop an understanding of the student's place in history by using timelines.

☐ Reflect on personal connections and changes of relationships over time by examining family trees, life lines, and photo albums.

ABILITY TO CONSERVE CONSTANCIES

Description

[Conservation of constancy is] the capacity of the individual to conserve the constancy of objects across variations in some of their attributes and dimensions. (Feuerstein, 1980, p. 85)

> There is more water in the glass than in the flat bowl.

The student has failed to understand the constancy of quantity.

Well-Developed Ability to Conserve Constancies

A well-developed ability to conserve constancies implies that students can

- Perceive that the essential property of an event or object stays the same despite changes in peripheral dimensions or orientation

- Identify an object even though variations in its attributes or appearance change (e.g., a person stays the same despite changes in clothing or expression)

- Understand that variations are produced by a transformation in presentation that can be reversed, and that the identity of the object remains the same (e.g., the quality of clay stays the same, regardless of whether it is rolled into a ball or formed into a sausage [quantity stays the same and shape differs])

Impaired Ability to Conserve Constancies

The student who experiences an impaired ability to conserve constancies may

- Lack an understanding of conservation and reversibility of numbers (e.g., cannot see that 3 + 2 = 5 is the same as 2 + 3 = 5)

- Have a tendency to focus only on the immediate appearance of an object without forming connections (episodic grasp of reality) or generalizing to the abstract (e.g., a glass viewed from the top looks like a circle while from the side it looks like a cylinder)

- Have difficulties perceiving similarities and differences either at a perceptual level (e.g., a square placed on an angle might be confused with a diamond) or at a conceptual level (e.g., a Maltese and a Great Dane might not both be considered dogs)

- Not be able to identify which relevant characteristics are conserved (e.g., is a kilogram of lead heavier than a kilogram of feathers?)

Various Occurrences

If conservation of constancy is impaired at the input phase (an inability to see similarities despite some differences), then at the elaboration phase the student will have difficulty forming categories (grouping according to similarities). This will result in inaccurate responses at the output phase.

Example

The student, when given two containers of different shapes that hold identical amounts, may not understand that despite the difference in the appearance of the containers, the volume they can hold is identical.

STRATEGIES

Examples	Strategies to Correct an Impaired Ability to Conserve Constancies

Meaning

The teacher facilitates conservation of quantity.

"Arrange these balls into as many different groups as possible. Does the number of balls stay the same?"

☐ Initiate students' self-learning by allowing them to manipulate concrete materials (e.g., measuring rods, puzzles, scales, blocks, modeling clay).

☐ Provide concrete experience with conservation of weight using a balance scale (e.g., ask the students if the two small bags of beans on the left-hand side of the scale weigh the same as the big bag of beans on the right-hand side of the scale).

☐ Word instructions to focus students' attention on constancies and changes, and similarities and differences, in weight, size, and shape.

Individuation

The teacher encourages creative interpretation.

"How many different ways can this problem be solved?"

☐ Explore how individuals stay the same despite changes in age, physical appearance, attitudes, values, financial status, and social position.

☐ Discuss how an individual's values stay the same despite changes in the roles he or she occupies in society (e.g., a career woman who becomes a mother).

☐ Challenge students to discover the concept that is common to answers that have been expressed in different ways.

☐ Invite students to demonstrate in as many ways as they can how to solve a problem, make a paper airplane, etc.

Transcendence

The teacher encourages application of conservation of quality.

"Which is more, four quarters or one dollar?"

☐ Relate tasks to everyday life (e.g., the value of money stays the same despite changes in the size of the coins).

☐ Practice measuring liquids and solids (e.g., eight ounces of sugar is the same as one cup).

☐ Demonstrate how the conservation of constancies can be used in different situations (e.g., ask students how to determine if the distance from New York to San Francisco depends on the speed of the vehicle one is traveling in).

☐ Bridge to perspective drawing in art or to seeing the same problem from different angles (e.g., the facts of an issue remain the same no matter what bias one has).

DATA GATHERING

Description

The dynamics of the orientation towards precision is based on a generalized need . . . (which) is established by a variety of strategies very early in the interactional processes between the child and his human environment. (Feuerstein, 1980, p. 87)

The student doesn't collect data accurately.

Precise and Accurate Data Gathering

The need for precise and accurate data gathering refers to the need to

- Develop an intrinsic need to be precise and accurate in gathering information
- Select only what is relevant to the accurate (appropriate or correct) processing of a problem once the need has been developed
- Use precise vocabulary (clearly stated and detailed) to ensure the economic and efficient "capturing" of information

Impaired Data Gathering

The student who exhibits impaired data gathering may

- Lack an understanding of the importance of being precise and accurate when gathering data
- Tend to produce work in which the data are neither precise (clearly stated and detailed) nor accurate (appropriate or correct)
- Present work that is incomplete, far too detailed, lacking logical form, or missing the salient points
- Be unable to evaluate whether data are missing or have been distorted
- Depend on the teacher's specific instructions and resources and be unable to draw on his or her own stored information or previous experience
- Lack the skills to research and extract information from a variety of sources even though the need has been developed

Various Occurrences

At the input phase, a differentiation can be made between perceptual difficulties in collecting data and the incomplete development of a need to be accurate and precise in data gathering. This can simultaneously affect cognitive processes, such as inaccuracies in comparison, at the elaboration phase. At the output phase, this affects the ability to communicate concepts clearly.

Example

When a student makes an error in class, he or she may not be aware of it due to a lack of an intrinsic need to check work for precision and accuracy.

STRATEGIES

Examples

Strategies to Correct Impaired Data Gathering

Meaning

The teacher clarifies sources of error.

"You got a D on your last essay because the following details were not relevant."

☐ Make explicit the benefits that are gained by being both precise and accurate when collecting information (e.g., the economic use of time and words will help others to better understand a message).

☐ Explain the difference between an accurate (correct) interpretation of a question and a precise (clearly stated) answer (e.g., an essay might contain many precisely stated facts that miss the point or are inaccurate in the context of the essay).

Transcendence

The teacher reinforces accurate attention to detail.

"Review what each one of you needs to do in order to make this event a success."

☐ Discuss how precision and accuracy have aided the overall expansion of human knowledge (e.g., careful scientific experimentation and observation).

☐ Show how misunderstandings can be avoided by accurate communication and precise planning.

☐ Illustrate how careful planning can increase the enjoyment of an event because all important aspects were considered beforehand (e.g., catering to everyone's needs at a party).

☐ Demonstrate how overlooking details can have universal repercussions that can lead to chaos and even death (e.g., missing a bolt on a nuclear reactor door).

Self-Regulation and Control of Behavior

The teacher draws attention to the consequences of errors.

"Be careful not to confuse a.m. and p.m. on the invitations as you did last time."

☐ Demonstrate strategies that can be used to capture, monitor, and check data collection (i.e., develop the need for a strategy to achieve precision and accuracy).

☐ Encourage the students to take responsibility for their actions (e.g., in making a cake, let the consequences of using two tablespoons instead of two teaspoons of cinnamon be experienced).

☐ Give feedback when errors are made due to a lack of attention to detail and misunderstanding of instructions, thereby developing a reciprocal need to be precise and accurate.

CONSIDER MORE THAN ONE SOURCE OF INFORMATION

Description

The use of two sources of information is a prerequisite of thinking because it is the basis of all relational thought processes. (Feuerstein, 1980, p. 88).

> This piece of the puzzle is the right color, but not the right shape.

The student needs to consider more than one source of information.

Well-Developed Capacity to Consider More Than One Source of Information

A well-developed capacity to consider more than one source of information refers to the ability to

- Think about two or more sources of information at the same time (e.g., to consider color, shape, and size when completing a jigsaw puzzle)
- Gather data from various sources (e.g., to refer to the teacher, experts, and the library as resources for a history project)
- Perceive an issue from different points of view
- Examine more than one aspect of a situation in order to see the relationship, connection, or links between them
- Use two elements as sources of data for comparison whenever a problem is confronted (e.g., to consider nutrition and availability of ingredients when planning a meal)

Impaired Capacity to Consider More Than One Source of Information

The student who experiences an impaired capacity to consider more than one source of information may

- Tend to focus on and take into account only one of a variety of dimensions or alternatives
- Consider only some of the information needed to complete an assignment or solve a problem
- Be unable to recall all the facts needed for completing a task
- Recall disjointed pieces of information and not be able to put them together to form a meaningful whole
- Engage in egocentric behavior (i.e., only see something from his or her point of view and have difficulty accommodating differing opinions)

Various Occurrences

The lack of, or impaired use of, two or more sources of information is a deficiency at the input phase. This will affect many of the cognitive processes at the elaboration phase (e.g., summative, comparative, and hypothetical thinking). This in turn will result in excessive trial-and-error behavior at the output phase, as well as an inability to present the problem in a multidimensional form.

Example

A student who focuses on some, but not all, of the facts will not be able to arrive at the correct answer in a story problem or a complicated math problem (e.g., calculating velocity when direction, displacement, and time all need to be considered simultaneously).

STRATEGIES

Examples

Strategies to Correct an Impaired Capacity to Consider More Than One Source of Information

Intentionality and Reciprocity

The teacher alerts the students to the need to consider two sources of information.

"In order to draw this graph accurately, we need to consider the x and the y values."

☐ Give students tasks to work on in which they are forced to use a variety of resources.

☐ Prolong exposure to stimuli to make various sources of information more conspicuous (e.g., say: "What else can you tell me about what you see?").

☐ Encourage students to be aware of, and attend to, various kinds of input (e.g., auditory, visual, tactile).

☐ Give explicit instructions to look for more sources of information.

☐ Highlight all the relevant factors that need to be considered (e.g., underlining, enlarged words, bright colors).

Meaning

The teacher shows how errors can be avoided by using all the appropriate information.

"That's only part of the answer. What else must we consider to predict the outcome?"

☐ Show how relative thinking can only come about when more than one source of information is considered (e.g., a poor man is considered rich in relation to a beggar).

☐ Provide feedback for inadequate answers (e.g., "You left out some information. Can you think of what it is?").

☐ Provide insight into the need for adequate consideration of all the data (e.g., "Don't jump to false conclusions.").

☐ Explain how all problem solving is based on considering various options (e.g., considering the pros and cons of a decision).

Transcendence

The teacher bridges the skill to related situations.

"A detective solving a murder case needs to piece together all the clues. In what other situations do we need to consider many aspects?"

☐ Show how nothing acts in isolation and that relationships can always be drawn among variables (e.g., the links in a food chain are affected by a number of environmental factors).

☐ Provide practice in solving problems in which two elements must be compared as sources of data (e.g., multiple-choice questions that include distractors).

☐ Encourage students to debate controversial issues from different points of view in order to develop empathy.

☐ Stimulate students to think of as many examples as possible when considering more than one source of evidence is vital (e.g., jury duty).

Work Page ·······························

Identify the Following Input Dysfunctions

1. Difficulty sequencing objects or events.

_____

2. Responding before the question or instructions have been completed.

_____

3. An inaccurate and incomplete perception of a situation.

_____

4. Confusing concepts such as "on," "under," "beside," "'front," "right," and "'left."

_____

5. Infrequent or inaccurate references to past or future events.

_____

6. Inability to follow verbal directions.

_____

7. Inability to recognize the same quantity of modeling clay when formed into different shapes.

_____

8. Responding only to the auditory input and ignoring the visual.

_____

Work Page ....

Match the Cognitive Dysfunctions

The Student Who

1. responds prematurely to the first and most obvious stimulus and lacks the self-control to approach a task systematically

2. has difficulty understanding instructions that have been communicated orally

3. has difficulty following a study timetable

4. has difficulty arranging the tens and ones into the proper columns

5. does not take time to focus clearly on all the necessary and relevant details

6. has difficulty considering all the alternatives of a multiple-choice question

7. cannot perceive that a square rotated on its axis is still a square

8. uses approximations and distorts certain dimensions when answering questions

Is Displaying

a. an impaired ability to use more than one source of information

b. impaired conservation of constancy

c. blurred and sweeping perception

d. impulsivity

e. an impaired need for precision

f. impaired spatial concept

g. impaired time concept

h. impaired verbal skills

Chapter **15**

Elaboration

I f some or all of the comments below about a student's thinking are overheard in the classroom, it is likely that the student is experiencing difficulty at the elaboration phase of the thinking process.

- "You haven't defined the problem"
- "Apply the old rule to this new example."
- "Remember the strategy we learned yesterday?"
- "You've missed an important clue."
- "How many examples did you find?"
- "Try to solve it without using a calculator."
- "Try to formulate a general rule from these examples."
- "Let's see what's similar and what's different here."
- "You haven't tested your hypothesis yet."
- "Give a logical explanation for your statement."
- "Try to see the connection between those two items."
- "You haven't elaborated or expanded on that idea."
- "You didn't plan that essay very well."

ELABORATION PHASE

Cognitive deficiencies can interact with each other, and with emotional and motivational factors, to make children school failures. But the precise nature of a child's deficiencies, resulting from inadequate Mediated Learning, are likely to be confused by teachers' and psychologists' preferences for gross descriptions of poor functioning. Feuerstein has attempted to map out, albeit fairly schematically, the act of thinking and the location of typical deficiencies within this act . . . to diagnose the root causes of a child's intellectual problems. Even minor impairments could, however, have a very significant

impact on children's thinking processes because of the knock-on effect onto other parts of the cognitive structure. A child who cannot be precise cannot compare effectively, and this affects the ability to classify, categorise, to draw analogies, and to make conclusions. (Sharron, 1987, p. 56)

The elaboration phase is the second step in the thinking process and is linked to the input phase—where data are gathered—and the output phase—where the answer is communicated.

At the elaboration phase, the gathered information is processed. It is the stage at which work is done, the task is undertaken, and the problems are solved. For example, the incoming information from the input phase is sorted, organized, analyzed, and tested in order to arrive at an answer or product that can be expressed at the output phase.

A student with difficulties at the elaboration phase may be unable to see when a problem exists and fail to use relevant clues to solve the problem. The student will not automatically compare objects, add items, or use what he or she has learned previously to form connections and links with new information. He or she may lack the ability or need to give a logical reason for his or her view, or think about things hypothetically. Such a student will not spontaneously make hypotheses or test them. This student may be disorganized and unable to expand or elaborate on an idea. Essentially, a student who has difficulties at the elaboration phase perceives things as separate and isolated, and fails to make connections between objects and events.

This chapter deals with such problems at the elaboration phase of thinking. A detailed explanation of how to identify each dysfunction is provided, and suggestions are made for correcting the dysfunction using Feuerstein's criteria of mediation.

Use this table to identify each child's cognitive dysfunction in the classroom illustration.

Elaboration	
Functions	**Dysfunctions**
Definition of the Problem	
Accurate	Inaccurate
Select Relevant Cues	
Ability to	Inability to
Engage in Spontaneous Comparative Behavior	
Ability to	Inability to
Mental Field	
Broad and Wide	Narrow and Limited
Spontaneous Summative Behavior	
Need for	Impaired Need for
Project Virtual Relations	
Ability to	Inability to
Logical Evidence	
Need for	Lack of need for
Internalize Events	
Ability to	Inability to
Inferential-Hypothetical Thinking	
Ability to Use	Impaired Ability to Use
Strategies for Hypothesis Testing	
Ability to Use	Impaired Ability to Use
Planning Behavior	
Need for	Lack of
Elaboration of Cognitive Categories	
Adequate	Impaired
Grasp of Reality	
Meaningful	Episodic

DEFINITION OF THE PROBLEM

Description

To perceive that a problem exists, a person must first establish a relationship among the various sources of information in the given data and then note that there is a discrepancy or incompatibility in the newly established relationship. (Feuerstein et al., 1986, p. 3.10)

The student is often unclear.

Accurate Definition of the Problem

An accurate definition of the problem refers to the ability to

- Sense that something is wrong and needs attention
- Identify the source or discrepancy that created the problem (i.e., clearly recognize and state the cause and nature of the problem)
- State all the factors that influence the problem and identify those that are incompatible

Inaccurate Definition of the Problem

The student who inaccurately defines a problem may

- Be unable to see incompatibility between sources of information (i.e., may not recognize that a problem exists)
- Have poor data-gathering skills and be unable to form relationships among things and think reflectively about them
- Demonstrate a lack of insight when assessing a situation
- Be insensitive to, and lack curiosity about, problems
- Have difficulty deciding on a course of action in response to a situation

---

Various Occurrences

Proficiency in all the functions at the input phase aids in the initial definition of a problem at the elaboration phase. This is an awareness of incongruous, incompatible, or missing elements in a situation; that is, there is disequilibrium. To fully understand the problem, one might need to continually return back to the input phase (e.g., to collect more data). A clear definition of the problem facilitates an accurate response at the output phase.

Example

A student with an inadequacy in experiencing or defining a problem may tend to be passive when faced with a task because he or she is unsure of what needs to be done. This student may be unable to continue working independently, may frequently ask that the task be reexplained, and might be unable to apply the concepts being taught.

STRATEGIES

Examples

Strategies to Correct Inaccurate Definition of a Problem

Intentionality and Reciprocity

The teacher focuses the problem for the students.

"What do you think you will be asked to do here?"

- ☐ Ask the students to describe in their own words how they perceive the problem.
- ☐ Return to the input phase to ensure that all data have been gathered with precision and accuracy.
- ☐ Arouse curiosity in passive students by asking questions relating to the activity.
- ☐ Supply students with problems in which they have to identify the incongruity in a set of circumstances.

Meaning

The teacher encourages identification of incongruity.

"Can you identify what's needed in order to be able to solve the problem?"

- ☐ Show how comparing, relating, and combining data can lead to a more precise definition of the problem.
- ☐ Explain how to search for and form relationships between bits of information so that the incongruity can be identified (e.g., comparison charts, categorization tables).
- ☐ Encourage students to perceive problems in terms of what caused them and to isolate factors that will be most influential in remedying them.

Self-Regulation and Control of Behavior

The teacher stimulates reflective thinking and analysis.

"What is the flaw in that argument?"

- ☐ Establish in students the habit of questioning incongruity or missing elements.
- ☐ Provide practice in finding contradictions in arguments.
- ☐ Encourage students to be actively involved in defining problems by analyzing a situation systematically and thinking logically (e.g., breaking problems down into smaller parts).

SELECT RELEVANT CUES

Description

[To select relevant cues] it is necessary first to define the specific goals [which will determine the person's] amount of focusing and the degree of relevance of each cue. (Feuerstein, 1980, p. 91)

The student is unable to extract the essential information.

Ability to Select Relevant Cues

The ability to select relevant cues implies that the student can

- Choose and use the correct and appropriate information needed to solve a problem
- Define the goal and select from a number of cues only those that are specifically relevant to meet the particular goal
- Decide what aspects will be useful in a particular situation
- View all options purposefully in order to differentiate between relevant and appropriate information, as opposed to irrelevant and inappropriate information

Impaired Ability to Select Relevant Cues

The student who has an impaired ability to select relevant cues may have difficulty

- Finding the main points of a text
- Extracting the moral of a story
- Sticking to the point in an argument, discussion, or debate
- Finding points to substantiate an argument
- Solving problems that require discrimination and elimination of irrelevant alternatives (e.g., multiple-choice answers, word problems)
- Learning large sections of material for tests and exams

Various Occurrences

An inability to gather data precisely and accurately in the input phase will result in difficulties in defining a problem in the elaboration phase. If a problem is not clearly understood, it will be difficult to select important and relevant cues for its solution. This will result in errors expressed in the output phase.

Example

A student who cannot eliminate certain cues and assign preference to others will ramble off the point in discussions and have difficulty solving problems. For example, if the class is discussing camels, such a student would relate a story about his or her dog. Or, if required to select the missing puzzle piece from a choice of six alternatives—all equal in size but differing in color and shape—he or she will be unable to see that size is irrelevant because such a student does not discriminate between the various alternatives.

STRATEGIES

Examples

Strategies to Correct an Inability to Select Relevant Cues

Meaning

The teacher encourages the use of mind maps.

"Make a mind map that will show all the important points at a glance."

☐ Encourage "purposeful perception" (i.e., observing items with the specific aim of comparing them according to relevant criteria in order to discard irrelevant items). For example:
  – Compare items according to relevant criteria and discard all that are different
  – Categorize them into groups and subgroups according to relevant cues
  – Organize items according to increasing size or chronological order

☐ Provide practice in identifying the main points of a text by encouraging students to ask "why" and "how" questions.

☐ Help students to discover the value of mind maps and flow charts in summarizing text.

Goal Planning

The teacher mediates the strategy for achieving a goal.

"Identify specifically all the things you need to do to achieve your goal."

☐ Encourage students to set clear goals when beginning a project, which will help focus attention on more specific information.

☐ Challenge students to describe their goals in their own words, which will help clarify thinking.

☐ Help students to identify the steps involved in achieving goals in order to establish a framework from which to select relevant cues.

Self-Regulation and Control of Behavior

The teacher encourages a methodical approach.

"What clues will help you to solve the problem?"

☐ Ensure that students understand the requirements of the task before beginning the activity (e.g., defining the essay topic before starting to write).

☐ Help to instill the habit of cross checking (e.g., checking that all the appropriate information has been accumulated before proceeding with a math exercise).

☐ Reinforce the need to control impulsivity and not rush through a task (e.g., in a reading or comprehension exercise, students must grasp the main idea of each paragraph before reading on).

ENGAGE IN SPONTANEOUS COMPARATIVE BEHAVIOR

Description

Spontaneous comparative behavior is . . . one of the most fundamental building blocks of higher cognitive processes and . . . enables . . . an individual to transcend his immediate perceptual experience and establish relationships. (Feuerstein, 1980, p. 39)

I can't decide which option to choose between these two.

The child's inability to spontaneously compare interferes with decision making.

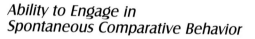

Ability to Engage in Spontaneous Comparative Behavior

An ability to engage in spontaneous comparative behavior implies that the student can

- Move from simply recognizing objects and events to establishing relationships among them
- Make automatic comparisons when approaching tasks and problems
- Spontaneously search for similarities and differences among items
- Organize and integrate discrete units of information into meaningful systems that are interrelated
- Use and modify the criteria of comparison dynamically to suit the problem

Inability to Engage in Spontaneous Comparative Behavior

The student who is unable to engage in spontaneous comparative behavior may

- Have an "episodic grasp of reality" in which items are viewed separately and as having no relationship to one another
- Have difficulty comparing two items (e.g., will describe one or the other item individually without mentioning the connection between the two)
- Have difficulty using adjectives such as "similar," "like," and "unlike" in spontaneous speech
- Have difficulty making decisions that involve the underlying skill of comparing (i.e., using relevant criteria to identify similarities and differences among items)
- Make sweeping generalizations about people or events without taking notice of individual differences

Various Occurrences

The ability to compare spontaneously is affected by accurate and thorough processes at the input phase. It is an important function of the elaboration phase because it is a prerequisite to forming relationships and linking items. As such, it is central to thinking and influences the way a response is communicated in the output phase.

Example

A student who lacks spontaneous comparative behavior will have difficulty with decision making because he or she will not be able to weigh the pros and cons of a situation (e.g., in a career choice).

STRATEGIES

Examples

Strategies to Correct an Inability to Engage in Spontaneous Comparative Behavior

Meaning

The teacher mediates a strategy for comparing.

"Let's determine the similarities and the differences between these two objects."

☐ Explain how comparisons are made by referring to both similarities and differences according to relevant and appropriate criteria.

☐ Show how relevant criteria of comparison will vary depending on the purpose of the comparison.

☐ Encourage students to "mentally overlap" two items to establish similarities and differences between them.

☐ Provide students with criteria or attributes according to which items may be compared (e.g., color—black/white, size—large/small).

☐ Show how a continuum can be used to illustrate degrees of comparison and opposites.

Transcendence

The teacher encourages continual application of comparison.

"In order to choose a future career you need to weigh all the pros and cons."

☐ Provide examples that students can use to practice the skill of comparison—both at home and in the classroom (e.g., compare characters in a novel; ads for a product; careers according to the criteria of job description, hours, pay; or offer different strategies for solving a problem).

☐ Show how the prosecution and the defense can win arguments using critical comparison of facts.

Optimistic Alternative

The teacher suggests that the student compare two alternatives before deciding.

"The only way to decide which method is better is to compare both."

☐ Encourage students to compare alternatives before decision making by
  - Creating two or three possible solutions
  - Listing the pros and cons for each
  - Reflecting on the most beneficial alternative for their need and adopting a positive view of the outcome

MENTAL FIELD

Description

This deficiency is evident in the limitation of the number of units of information that are manipulated or processed simultaneously [or] . . . the short blanket effect, i.e., uncovering one's shoulders when covering one's feet and vice versa. (Feuerstein et al., 1986, p. 3.11)

> I've learned the work, but I just can't seem to remember it later.

The student's narrow and limited mental field affects his ability to recall.

Broad and Wide Mental Field

A broad and wide mental field refers to the ability to

- Retain a number of units of information in order to mentally manipulate them
- Focus on, retain, and use two or more sources of information simultaneously
- Recall bits of information that have been previously stored
- Recall relevant information from past experiences
- Coordinate information from a wide variety of sources

Narrow and Limited Mental Field

The student who has a narrow and limited mental field may

- Be reluctant to engage in the act of trying to commit facts to memory (i.e., not take responsibility for actively integrating and storing information)
- Have poor short-term memory recall (i.e., experience difficulty in remembering bits of information recently stored)
- Have poor long-term memory (i.e., experience difficulty retrieving information that has been stored in the memory over a period of time)
- Recall facts episodically (i.e., remember facts on one day but not on another)
- Have difficulty coordinating facts from more than one source of information (i.e., be unable to associate or link information in order to make it meaningful)

Various Occurrences

Narrowness of the mental field usually manifests itself as a memory problem, which will affect all three phases of cognition. In the input phase, there is a lack of the need to use two or more sources of information simultaneously; at the elaboration phase, this results in an inability to remember or extract information from multiple sources; at the output phase, this manifests itself as poor recall.

Example

A student who has a narrow and limited mental field may be unable to remember facts when trying to study for exams. This student can remember parts of an event but not all of it. The student may also have difficulty remembering the details of a place he or she has visited, or a story he or she has read.

STRATEGIES

Examples	Strategies to Correct a Narrow and Limited Mental Field

Intentionality and Reciprocity

The teacher encourages short-term recall.

"Tell me about what we've just discussed."

☐ Use magnification (make stimulus larger) and color (make color brighter) to aid poor visual memory.

☐ Use amplification (make stimulus louder and clearer) to aid auditory memory.

☐ Ask students to recall or re-explain what you have just said—start with short passages and build up to longer ones.

Meaning

The teacher mediates a strategy to aid memorization.

"Let's group this information into categories to help you remember."

☐ Organize information appropriately to make sure it is understood before committing it to memory.

☐ Break information down into manageable chunks ("chunking") (e.g., 463921 becomes 46—39—21; this can be done with letters, words, and information).

☐ Make picture cards of a sequence of events that the student must assemble (e.g., getting ready for bed).

☐ Use categorization and grouping as techniques to aid memorization.

☐ Use revisualization and association techniques that help make information more interesting and therefore easier to remember.

☐ Show students the value of processing information through different modalities in order to aid recall (e.g., by drawing pictures or diagrams, acting, singing, and using mind maps).

Self-Regulation and Control of Behavior

The teacher encourages self-monitoring of behavior by instilling good habits.

"Read, write, and repeat in order to help you remember information."

☐ Move students from passive acceptance learning to actively constructing, understanding, and integrating information in order to commit it to memory.

☐ Encourage students to retell a story in order to facilitate meaningful memorization.

☐ Encourage the use of constant repetition to improve recall of information stored over time.

☐ Encourage students to monitor improvements in their memory by checking (e.g., "How many objects in the box can you remember today?").

SPONTANEOUS SUMMATIVE BEHAVIOR

Description

This deficiency reflects the lack of an orientation to sum up reality as a part of one's interaction with stimuli. Summative behavior makes use of both absolute and relative quantification in grouping, comparing, subtracting and even multiplying events. (Feuerstein et al., 1986, p. 3.12)

I never thought about how many children are in our class.

The student doesn't relate to his world in terms of number.

Need for Spontaneous Summative Behavior

The need for spontaneous summative behavior refers to the ability to

- Concern oneself with the "how many" of things around us
- Add numbers, objects, and events with a clear goal in mind
- Organize one's interaction with stimuli with the aim of grouping, summating, and drawing conclusions from the data
- Quantify events, ideas, and materials in order to compare, evaluate, and put them into perspective
- Extract the underlying concept from a summary of information

Impaired Need for Spontaneous Summative Behavior

The student who has an impaired need for spontaneous summative behavior may

- Not deem it necessary to quantify anything (e.g., respond to the question of "How many?" with "I don't know . . . lots")
- "List" data without the need to make meaningful relationships or assimilate them into an appropriate schema
- Count and add in a rote fashion without a true understanding of underlying number concepts
- Be unable to apply concepts because of an inability to summarize data in order to extract underlying concepts

---

Various Occurrences

At the input phase, stimuli are perceived episodically and in isolation. If this does not occur at the elaboration phase, there is no need to form relationships between numbers, acts, or events in order to sum up information. The lack of an imposed schema makes the information difficult to communicate in the output phase.

Example

In learning simple addition, the student will push counters together to arrive at a correct answer by "counting" each counter separately, rather than by relating each number to another in terms of size, order, reversibility, class, and part-whole relationships. The student is thus unable to gain an in-depth understanding of the underlying concepts implicit in addition.

STRATEGIES

Examples	Strategies to Correct an Impaired Need for Spontaneous Summative Behavior

Meaning

The teacher calls for the underlying math concepts.

"Is this getting bigger or smaller? Are we adding or subtracting?"

- ☐ Avoid mechanical computations that mask full understanding of underlying concepts (e.g., failure to sum up the relationship between mathematical processes, such as multiplication is recurring addition).
- ☐ Practice summarizing a subject by creating an overview of the area of study and relating different aspects of the topic.
- ☐ Promote active learning of addition and subtraction by direct exposure to stimuli and allow students to discover answers rather than providing them (e.g., use concrete manipulative materials, like units and blocks, life-size number lines, fingers).
- ☐ Provide students with study skills to summarize and relate facts meaningfully (e.g., finding main ideas; finding details; sequencing facts; relating details of cause and effect; predicting outcomes; drawing conclusions).

Intentionality and Reciprocity

The teacher affirms a summative response.

"Yes, you can group these together in order to add them."

- ☐ Present pieces of information to students in a way that suggests the relationship among the pieces.
- ☐ Verbally draw students' attention to the need for summative behavior by constantly requesting quantifying processes, such as counting, subtracting, and adding.
- ☐ Acknowledge responses when they demonstrate summative behavior.

Transcendence

The teacher elaborates a strategy for summarizing and relating facts.

"Let's summarize the causes of the French Revolution by relating all the facts in a creative pattern or mind map."

- ☐ Help students to summarize facts about a new content area so that they are enumerated and meaningfully related to each other, as well as related to knowledge already stored in memory.
- ☐ Provide examples that students can use to practice collecting and summarizing facts in order to investigate, draw conclusions, and make decisions (e.g., buying a car, house, appliance; planning an outing or trip; examining the pros and cons of a job).

PROJECT VIRTUAL RELATIONSHIPS

Description

The lack of need to seek relationships is an operational expression of an episodic grasp of reality. The deduction of a relationship from among all those that are virtually possible requires the establishment of a link (or connection) among objects and/or events. (Feuerstein et al., 1986, 3.15)

The student experiences difficulty applying a concept in a novel situation.

Ability to Project Virtual Relationships

The ability to project virtual relationships implies that the student can

- Form relationships between seemingly isolated events, which involves
  - Applying previously learned rules and concepts to new situations
  - Restructuring relationships to make meaningful, new connections
- Bridge thinking skills to form relationships in a variety of situations that exist "virtually" or "potentially"
- Recognize a change in the relationship when one or more stimuli are altered
- Restructure existing connections between objects or events in order to solve new problems

Inability to Project Virtual Relationships

The inability to project virtual relationships implies that the student may

- Be unable to apply a concept learned in one area to different subject matter (e.g., not realize that adding apples is the same as adding pears)
- Tend to stick to a fixed relationship even when the stimuli have demanded that the relationship change (e.g., apply the theorem learned for a triangle to a square, a case in which the sides and angles have changed)

Various Occurrences

At the input phase, an episodic grasp of reality may mean that the fundamental relationship is not seen. This impacts the elaboration phase, resulting in the student's inability to apply known concepts to formulate new relationships, look for parallels, or see analogies. As a result, communication of information at the output phase is meaningless and unrelated.

Example

In the classroom, the student will be passive. This student will not have the need to apply previously learned skills to new information to make it meaningful. The student will then experience information as isolated and separate and will be unable to bridge relationships to new situations. He or she will fail to see that doing subtraction in school is the same as getting change when buying something in a store.

STRATEGIES

Examples	Strategies to Correct an Inability to Project Virtual Relationships

Meaning

The teacher gives reasons for restructuring a relationship.

"This algebra problem cannot be solved accurately unless you extend the relationship between x and y to include z."

☐ Provide insight and awareness into the limitations of passively accepting a relationship without testing it in a new situation.

☐ Show how studying is facilitated when new information is grouped and linked to existing knowledge.

☐ Instill a need to question any new input that seems meaningless or unrelated to a topic.

☐ Show how problem solving can be made more expedient by using previously integrated concepts and reconfiguring them to suit the situation.

Transcendence

The teacher provides opportunities for bridging to new situations.

"How would you modify the method of sorting to incorporate these new items?"

☐ Provide practice in applying a skill to a variety of tasks (e.g., grouping by size, number, name, function).

☐ Allow students to form new links based on relationships between events in everyday life situations (e.g., generalize the operation of making a phone call to various types of phones).

☐ Provide opportunities that encourage the students to extend or modify a relationship in order to achieve a result (e.g., "You proved that all the substances formed salt crystals; what would you do to liquefy them?").

Competence

The teacher practices spontaneous application of a concept to a new situation.

"Well done! You have shown how following a plan can be used to solve both a math problem and organize a dinner party."

☐ Develop increasingly difficult tasks in which new configurations have to be formed before success is achieved.

☐ Reward students for adapting relative values or relationships to suit new tasks.

☐ Praise students for the spontaneous use of skills such as grouping, comparing, and categorizing in novel situations.

LOGICAL EVIDENCE

Description

A lack of need for logical evidence does not necessarily reflect on a deficiency to operate logically, because the child's responses sometimes do demonstrate logical understanding. Rather, the inconsistency frequently observed in the child's responses may be ascribed to a faulty need system in which logical evidence is not prominent and pertinent. (Feuerstein, 1980, p. 96)

The student doesn't search for explanations.

Need for Logical Evidence

A need for logical evidence refers to the ability to

- Internalize the desire to challenge and question the way things are
- Seek evidence to support or confirm the validity of statements, facts, and events
- Seek logical consistency in order to discover or resolve a contradiction
- Generate questions, seek answers, and communicate explanations
- Actively seek a solution once a problem is faced (when disequilibrium is experienced)
- Automatically want to isolate the inconsistency in a sequence of events (e.g., enjoy finding the "odd man out")

Lack of Need for Logical Evidence

The student who displays a lack of need for logical evidence may

- Not be able to support judgments, responses, or assertions with adequate explanations
- Display a "so what" or passive acceptance attitude when facing problems
- Not instigate an active search for a solution although a problem is evident
- Be able to display some logical understanding but fail to apply logic to finding solutions
- Remain inconsistent in formulating opinions
- Respond to situations prematurely or irrationally
- Be easily persuaded to adopt others' solutions to problems without thinking them through

Various Occurrences

The student who displays a passive, or acceptant, attitude to information at the input phase will have an inadequate need for pursuing logical evidence and supporting statements and judgments at the elaboration phase. This may often result in poor communication at the output phase (e.g., the student answers "because" when asked "why").

Example

Students may often present inadequate reasons for maintaining an opinion, or reach conclusions based on scant and/or contradictory evidence.

STRATEGIES

Examples	Strategies to Correct a Lack of Need for Logical Evidence

Meaning

The teacher asks for justification for an argument.

"In order to convince me that you are right you need to prove it to me."

☐ Actively mediate the importance of being able to supply appropriate and logical reasons for opinions or events (e.g., overcoming prejudices).

☐ Provide graphic examples of the consequences of accepting ideas or conclusions without examining them (e.g., the consequences of buying a product solely on the basis of an advertisement).

☐ Explain the importance of evidence in the judicial system (e.g., how guilt or innocence may be determined only by pursuing facts that have a logical base).

Transcendence

The teacher develops the need for logical evidence in many different contexts.

"In what ways do doctors, lawyers, and journalists all rely on logical evidence?"

☐ Encourage students to argue and debate issues from various perspectives, bringing evidence to bear for all possible opinions.

☐ Provide opportunities for students to experience the many ways in which logical evidence is applied (e.g., in the courts, science, debate, law making, negotiation, decision making).

☐ Explore opportunities to reach decisions based on logical evidence that may impact the students' lives (e.g., school rules regarding litter, loitering, graffiti).

☐ Encourage the students to find or research supportive evidence in order to explain an occurrence (e.g., why a fire started or an accident occurred).

Individuation

The teacher accepts individual responses based on their logic.

"I accept both Theresa's and Jane's answers because they both justified their responses logically."

☐ Present controversial topics and allow the students to formulate their own opinions, giving logical reasons to support their views.

☐ Acknowledge the individual's right to different views, as long as they are logically justified.

☐ Encourage students to adopt the pursuit of logical evidence in solving personal problems rather than relying solely on an emotional response.

INTERNALIZE EVENTS

Description

This dysfunction is apparent in the pervasiveness of task-bound, concrete behavior. (Feuerstein et al., 1986, p. 3.15)

The student cannot solve problems mentally.

Ability to Internalize Events

An ability to internalize events implies that the student can

- Assimilate and accommodate information in order to make generalizations
- Think in the abstract (without concrete aids) (e.g., use representations such as signs, symbols, and concepts to process data)
- Mentally manipulate information and concepts that have been stored (internalized)
- Use stored information to think about and solve problems

Inability to Internalize Events

The student who experiences an inability to internalize events may

- Rely heavily on concrete aids and sensorial input (e.g., use blocks and fingers for counting)
- Be unable to hold on to or use various sources of information
- Be unable to solve problems "in his or her head"
- Show poor spontaneous concept formation (e.g., have difficulty formulating a conclusion)
- Be unable to link present events with past and future events (e.g., be located in the here and now)
- Have difficulty completing tasks that rely on previously internalized processes (e.g., knowing tables for multidigit multiplication)

Various Occurrences

At the input phase, the student relies strongly on concrete cues, which results in limited representational thinking. Cognitive components like planning, processing, and projecting are then restricted at the elaboration phase. This results in an inability to communicate ideas or solutions in an abstract way at the output phase.

Example

The student will need to physically manipulate stimuli when solving problems and will be unable to think hypothetically—he or she will have to literally "place his or her hand in the fire to know that fire burns"; the student cannot think of heat in an abstract way or draw on past experiences of fire.

STRATEGIES

Examples	Strategies to Correct an Inability to Internalize Events

Competence

The teacher encourages the move from the concrete to the abstract.

"Add two to three without using blocks this time."

☐ Initially provide the use of concrete aids and, as the students' performance improves, gradually reduce dependency on aids, thus preventing anxiety (e.g., "First use your counters and then try the next example without them.").

☐ Encourage visualization by allowing students to close their eyes and "see, feel, and move" objects in their head as a method of understanding and integrating information.

Self-Regulation and Control of Behavior

The teacher encourages the students to learn from past errors.

"Think now—don't make the same mistakes as last time."

☐ Hide ready-made answers and encourage anticipation of an answer through questioning and probing (e.g., "What do you think is going to happen next?").

☐ Provide oral instructions, step by step, and encourage the students to think through the process.

☐ Encourage the students to verbalize the steps or rules required to complete a task before attempting it.

☐ Encourage reflective thinking by monitoring events after they have happened.

Transcendence

The teacher encourages interiorized planning.

"What do we need to do in order to make these puppets?"

☐ Provide the students with the relevant vocabulary to generalize, categorize, and classify information in order to develop an understanding of concepts.

☐ Emphasize relationships between pieces of information in order to help the students to draw from past experiences when solving a problem.

☐ Provide practice in solving everyday problems (e.g., receiving change, paying bills, organizing an outing).

INFERENTIAL-HYPOTHETICAL THINKING

Description

The proposition "if . . . , then" is the expression of hypothetical thinking . . . and (requires) a readiness to seek alternatives by which to explain phenomena. (Feuerstein et al., 1986, p. 3.13)

The student engages in "if . . . , then" thinking.

Ability to Use Inferential-Hypothetical Thinking

Inferential-hypothetical thinking refers to the ability to

- Make valid generalizations and inferences based on a number of experiences
- Generate a number of possible theories based on evidence, which will be tested at a later stage
- Draw a conclusion from a number of similar examples (e.g., "If fire burns wood, then my hand will probably burn when I put it into the fire.")

Restricted Use of Inferential-Hypothetical Thinking

The student who experiences a restricted use of inferential-hypothetical thinking may

- Be unable to link events or see similarities among things in order to make generalizations and inferences
- View the world as disconnected and have difficulty drawing conclusions
- Not "see" other alternatives or explore other possibilities to explain phenomena
- Not look for evidence to create a hypothesis

Various Occurrences

Clear and accurate perception, precise and accurate data gathering, and the ability to consider many sources of information at the input phase are essential for inferential-hypothetical thinking. At the elaboration phase, theories and generalizations are formed based on similarities in the evidence. At the output phase, the hypothesis is precisely and accurately explained using adequate expressive verbal tools.

Example

A student who manifests a restricted use of inferential-hypothetical thinking might not be able to find alternative ways to get home after missing his or her bus. The student is unable to see the link between catching the bus and other means of getting home; he or she cannot reflect back to similar past experiences in order to generate possible solutions. This student does not engage in "if . . . , then" thinking, that is, "If I missed the bus, then I could take a taxi, walk, phone home, . . ."

STRATEGIES

Examples	Strategies to Correct Restricted Use of Inferential-Hypothetical Thinking

Meaning

The teacher shows the value of generating a hypothesis.

"If Madame Curie hadn't hypothesized about radiation, x-rays would never have been discovered."

☐ Demonstrate how new conclusions can be drawn by considering existing information.

☐ Explain how developing hypotheses forms the basis for creating links and insights crucial for the exploration of new ideas.

☐ Explain how making connections between objects or events helps generate viable propositions or theories in problem solving.

Competence

The teacher provides practice using the "If . . . , then" formula.

"If 10, 20, 30, and 40 are all divisible by 2, then 80 should also be divisible by 2."

☐ Provide students with experience in generating hypotheses based on a number of proven situations (e.g., "If these three-sided shapes are triangles, then those three-sided shapes must also be triangles.").

☐ In order to make what appears to be complex more accessible, show students how to make inferences from commonalties in things they see (e.g., that multiplication is repeated addition).

☐ Provide practice using the formula "if . . . , then" (e.g., "If cork, wood, and styrofoam all float, then they are all less dense than water.").

Individuation

The teacher promotes critical thinking in justifying hypotheses.

"What other examples can you give to support your hypothesis?"

☐ Explore brainstorming as a means for generating original and diverse hypotheses (i.e., ideas that will be tested or validated at a later date).

☐ Encourage students to justify their own hypotheses by supporting them with numerous examples and logical evidence.

☐ Ask students to make explicit the thinking process that enabled them to formulate their conclusions.

STRATEGIES FOR HYPOTHESIS TESTING

Description

In hypothesis testing, competing possibilities must be kept in mind, tested and either accepted or rejected before a valid hypothesis is finally selected from among them. (Feuerstein et al., 1986, p. 3.13)

The student wants to test out a hypothesis.

Ability to Use Strategies for Hypothesis Testing

The ability to use strategies for hypothesis testing implies that the student can

- Devise a suitable method for assessing a particular hypothesis (e.g., research, experimentation, practical experience)
- Analyze and evaluate the validity of the process used in formulating a hypothesis (e.g., check that extraneous information was not included)
- Compare and contrast all possible theories and identify which hypothesis is most appropriate in a given situation
- Systematically examine a number of alternative hypotheses and, by a process of elimination, select the most viable options

Impaired Ability to Use Strategies for Hypothesis Testing

The student who experiences an impaired ability to use strategies for hypothesis testing may

- Be unable to devise or select the most appropriate method of testing a particular hypotheses (e.g., rely on guesses or estimates rather than on empirical evidence)
- Use unsystematic or inefficient approaches to testing alternative hypotheses (e.g., walk the distance to validate the predicted shortest route instead of using a map)
- Be unable to make suitable choices because the alternative hypotheses have not been successfully tested (e.g., experience difficulty in answering multiple-choice questions and be impulsive in selecting the most valid response)

Various Occurrences

Clear and accurate perception, precise and accurate data gathering, and the ability to consider many sources of information at the input phase are essential for inferential-hypothetical thinking. At the elaboration phase, theories and generalizations are formed based on similarities in the evidence. At the output phase, the hypothesis is precisely and accurately explained using adequate expressive verbal tools.

Example

A student who manifests a restricted use of inferential-hypothetical thinking might not be able to find alternative ways to get home after missing his or her bus. The student is unable to see the link between catching the bus and other means of getting home; he or she cannot reflect back to similar past experiences in order to generate possible solutions. This student does not engage in "if . . . , then" thinking, that is, "If I missed the bus, then I could take a taxi, walk, phone home, . . ."

STRATEGIES

Examples

Strategies to Correct an Impaired Ability to Use Strategies for Hypothesis Testing

Self-Regulation and Control of Behavior

The teacher encourages the verbalization of strategies.

"Explain how you could validate your hypothesis."

☐ Provide opportunities to establish the habit of checking or testing alternatives (e.g., in a science experiment, test whether or not various substances will dissolve as predicted).

☐ Challenge the students to develop their own strategies for efficient hypothesis testing in order to prioritize alternative solutions.

☐ Encourage students to verbalize their strategy for hypothesis testing as an aid to working systematically.

Meaning

The teacher reinforces the need to use a strategy to evaluate alternatives.

"How can you tell which of your ideas will build the strongest bridge?"

☐ Demonstrate the value of using a strategy for hypothesis testing (e.g., using the same set of questions to test a number of hypotheses can help decision making).

☐ Show how a problem can be solved effectively by choosing the most suitable method of hypothesis testing (e.g., refer to documented evidence instead of undertaking time-consuming experiments).

Self-Change

The teacher refers to the process of hypothesis testing in self-growth.

"What were you thinking about before you decided to choose that career option?"

☐ Develop strategies to evaluate a set of hypotheses resulting in self-change (e.g., list the pros and cons of a hypothesis involving achieving independence, such as getting a job, borrowing money, living with a friend).

☐ Help students monitor self-change by recalling previously used hypothesis testing strategies (e.g., "I thought very carefully about X, Y, and Z and decided to choose Z because. . . .").

☐ Discuss how reliably testing hypotheses, rather than guessing, can result in self-change (e.g., using empirical testing to overcome self-doubt, such as vocational tests rather than subjective opinions in assessing one's aptitude for a career).

PLANNING BEHAVIOR

Description

Planning behavior involves setting goals . . . and differentiating between the goals and the means by which they can be attained. The steps by which to reach an objective must be detailed, ordered in time, and evaluated in terms of their feasibility, economy and efficiency. (Feuerstein, 1980, p. 99)

The student fails to generate a plan.

Need for Planning Behavior

The need for planning behavior refers to the ability to

- See the value of setting long-term and short-term goals
- Project into the future in order to plan ahead
- Formulate goals and state how they can be attained
- Construct and follow a plan in order to achieve goals or solve problems
- Identify the specific steps involved in following a plan
- Understand the importance of working systematically and logically when executing a plan
- Modify courses of action in terms of their economy and efficiency

Lack of Need for Planning Behavior

The student who experiences a lack of planning behavior may

- Be unable to delay gratification in order to plan and invest in the long term
- Rush into a situation impulsively without prior planning
- Not see the need to plan but rather live in the "here and now," solving only immediate problems
- Be unaware of the techniques and processes involved in setting, seeking, and reaching goals
- Be unable to explicitly state the steps involved in solving a problem
- Struggle to follow a plan

Various Occurrences

Impulsivity and an episodic grasp of reality at the input phase cause difficulties in setting goals, as well as planning the steps to attaining the goals at the elaboration phase. This will result in trial-and-error behavior, which will in turn impair output responses.

Example

Children who live under very poor or dangerous environmental conditions and experience a hand-to-mouth existence do not develop the need to plan for the future or predict and invest in the long term. Their environment forces them to live in the "here and now," in which planning ahead is unnecessary. Similarly, an impulsive or overindulged child whose needs are immediately satisfied does not develop the attitude or skills required for planning ahead and delaying immediate gratification.

STRATEGIES

Examples

Strategies to Correct a Lack of Planning Behavior

Goal Planning

The teacher mediates a strategy for goal planning.

"We need a plan for this difficult problem. Let's define our objective."

☐ Model goal-directed behavior (e.g., set clear goals for each lesson and state the steps involved in achieving the goal).

☐ Give students a strategy for devising a plan, such as the following:
  - Define your objectives
  - Gather the information
  - Consider the rules
  - Plan the strategy and starting point
  - Check that the objectives have been met

Self-Regulation and Control of Behavior

The teacher provides reasons for delaying gratification and planning ahead.

"If you don't eat all of your lunch now, you will be hungry in the afternoon."

☐ Encourage perseverance and patience in pursuing goals.

☐ Develop in students an intrinsic locus of control and an autonomous attitude to their destiny (taking responsibility for their own lives).

☐ Show how breaking long-term projects down into smaller parts and systematic stages makes a task more manageable.

☐ Help students to set priorities when planning ahead.

☐ Encourage impulsive students to delay gratification by showing the value of investing in the long term.

☐ Show students how to monitor and evaluate whether their goals have been achieved and how to modify their approach accordingly.

Individuation

The teacher encourages students to set and plan their own goals.

"You need to clarify your long-term career goals in order to choose the courses to take before high school graduation."

☐ Foster the need to set realistic goals.

☐ Encourage students to identify their needs and modify and adjust goals accordingly.

☐ Encourage students to evaluate and review their plans in terms of time and ability.

☐ Explore with students ways in which their different dreams and hopes for the future may be realized through effective planning behavior.

ELABORATION OF COGNITIVE CATEGORIES

Description

A lack of verbal skills may severely affect a child's ability to elaborate certain cognitive operations. The absence of a specific verbal code to designate certain attributes of an object will keep the child bound to specific tasks that he can handle on a concrete level and may impair his ability to generalize the same operation to tasks differing in content and complexity (Feuerstein, 1980, p. 82)

The student has difficulty extending an idea.

Adequate Elaboration of Cognitive Categories	*Impaired Elaboration of Cognitive Categories*
An adequate elaboration of cognitive categories refers to the ability to	The student who experiences an impaired elaboration of cognitive categories may
■ Move from a concrete example to an abstract understanding using language as a tool ■ Link a verbal label to its underlying concept (e.g., explore the meaning of a word like "conscience") ■ Discover, label, and verbalize underlying principles ■ "Think out loud" when working through an activity ■ Elaborate verbally on how gathered data can be organized into relevant categories	■ Lack the correct label for a particular object, sequence, relationship, or concept ■ Have difficulty moving from a concrete task to the underlying abstract principle ■ Be unable to express him- or herself and "think through" his or her approach to tasks ■ Have difficulty explaining concepts in great depth due to limited expressive or receptive vocabulary ■ Be unable to generalize a cognitive skill to similar tasks (e.g., may be able to compare two blocks but cannot use the same criteria to compare other objects)

Various Occurrences

This cognitive function relates to the link between language and thought. It refers to the vital role that language plays in defining a mental operation in abstract thinking. A lack of verbal tools (vocabulary) and an inability to use several sources of information simultaneously at the input phase will limit abstract thinking at the elaboration phase. This results in an impaired ability to verbalize and generalize a mental operation and apply it in similar situations at the output phase.

Example

In the classroom, the student will only feel comfortable with activities he or she can physically manipulate and will have difficulties describing what he or she is doing. The student will be unable to apply a rule learned on an easy example to a more difficult example and will have difficulty grouping related items into categories.

STRATEGIES

Examples

Strategies to Correct an Impaired Elaboration of Cognitive Categories

Intentionality and Reciprocity

The teacher provides correct labels to describe a mental process.

"When we compare, we look for what is the same and what is different."

☐ Ask students to explain abstract concepts such as love, hate, or prejudice in terms of how they view or think about them.

☐ Provide the students with the vocabulary necessary to describe cognitive operations, such as
  – Labeling objects—square, triangle
  – Describing relationships—similar, different

☐ Model "thinking out loud" and describe strategies for solving problems.

Meaning

The teacher provides reasons for applying thinking skills.

"To understand how the body functions, we need to break it down into various parts. This is called analysis."

☐ Explain the reasons for using mental processes to facilitate the move from concrete to abstract thinking (e.g., the purpose of analysis).

☐ Provide practice in understanding the mental processes involved in analyzing, synthesizing, comparing, categorizing, making inductions and deductions, etc.

☐ Challenge students to discover the value of being able to solve a problem abstractly without physically doing it (e.g., it saves time and energy, it is not dependent on physical props, it is essential for hypothetical thinking).

Transcendence

The teacher encourages the application of a strategy.

"You did a good job grouping those shapes. Now let's see if you can use the same rules to group these animals."

☐ Provide practice for applying a concept using varied and difficult examples (e.g., find superordinate and subordinate categories when classifying information).

☐ Show how a principle or operation can be used in related situations.

☐ Ask students to generate examples of how they would use a specific strategy to solve problems in their home, classroom, and everyday life.

GRASP OF REALITY

Description

Grasping the world episodically means that each object or event is experienced in isolation without any attempt to relate or link it to previous anticipated experiences in space or time. (Feuerstein, 1980, p. 102)

The student cannot see the connections.

Meaningful Grasp of Reality

Meaningful grasp of reality refers to the ability to

- Link information into a meaningful and comprehensible whole by actively finding relationships between items and events (e.g., by organizing, ordering, summating, comparing)
- Anticipate and predict consequences, establish cause-and-effect relationships, and see the implications of an action
- Internalize a need to adopt an active approach to information (e.g., make meaningful connections), as passivity may be considered a central cause of an episodic grasp of reality
- Control the impulsive urge to react, thus giving oneself time to come to a reasonable understanding of the problem

Episodic Grasp of Reality

The student who experiences an episodic grasp of reality may

- See the world as a series of disconnected, separate events that bear little relation to each other
- Need to revert to concrete experiences
- Have difficulty linking cause and effect or seeing consequences of actions
- Have difficulty placing an event into a category because each event is experienced as different and similarities to other events are not perceived
- Experience difficulty with concept formation, abstract reasoning, and integration of new material

Various Occurrences

This cognitive function relates to the link between language and thought. It refers to the vital role that language plays in defining a mental operation in abstract thinking. A lack of verbal tools (vocabulary) and an inability to use several sources of information simultaneously at the input phase will limit abstract thinking at the elaboration phase. This results in an impaired ability to verbalize and generalize a mental operation and apply it in similar situations at the output phase.

Example

In the classroom, the student will only feel comfortable with activities he or she can physically manipulate and will have difficulties describing what he or she is doing. The student will be unable to apply a rule learned on an easy example to a more difficult example and will have difficulty grouping related items into categories.

STRATEGIES

Examples

Strategies to Correct an Episodic Grasp of Reality

Meaning

The teacher establishes relationships.

"Addition and multiplication are both ways of increasing quantity."

- ☐ Give reasons for finding similarities and differences as a strategy for grouping items and making connections.
- ☐ Present tasks in which students are required to find a unifying concept (e.g., "How can I put all these blocks together?").
- ☐ Explore the idea of the interconnection of parts to the whole (e.g., how pollution affects life on the planet).
- ☐ Illustrate the impact of treating things in isolation and not "digging deeper" (e.g., repairing a crack in the wall without looking for its cause).

Sense of Belonging

The teacher expands the concept and importance of understanding relationships.

"Let's draw a family tree to trace how all your ancestors are connected."

- ☐ Explain how exploring relationships within our culture enables us to understand our own experiences in growing up in this world.
- ☐ Show how forming valid links regarding our place in the world allows us to add and find increasingly more complex and subtle relationships, which leads to our growth in understanding the self.
- ☐ Make explicit the idea that finding our roots and appreciating our relationships is a creative and dynamic act and is central to an individual's need to order what may seem like a chaotic, disordered, and unpredictable world.

Novelty and Challenge

The teacher challenges the students to look for a cause and effect.

"What do you think caused the extinction of dinosaurs?"

- ☐ Model an openness to "new" links while guiding the students to make valid judgments, thus keeping alive their motivation to try.
- ☐ Present tasks requiring insight into cause and effect at a level that challenges the students (e.g., in the game Clue, who killed Miss Scarlet, in which room, and with what weapon?).
- ☐ Develop the students' natural curiosity as to why things happen by asking them to provide reasons for phenomena (e.g., "Why do stars twinkle?").

Work Page ....

Identify the Following Elaboration Dysfunctions

1. Inability to perceive relationships among objects and events.

2. Difficulty explaining in words the abstract principle underlying a concrete task.

3. Inability to support a statement or justify a position.

4. Only checks back with the model example when specifically asked to do so.

5. Difficulty grasping the disequilibrium that exists in a given situation.

6. Lack of orientation to quantify or sum up stimuli as part of a need to organize information.

7. Lack of a need to restructure relationships to form new connections (that potentially exist between stimuli).

8. Inability to extract from the rule the answers to hypothetical examples.

9. Inability to combine and link units of information in order to retain them in long-term memory.

10. Inability to set goals that are located both temporally and spatially at a given distance from the "here and now."

11. Inability to represent in the mind's eye an object without having it present (i.e., being concrete bound).

12. Cannot eliminate certain cues and assign preferences to others in solving problems.

13. Cannot construct a general rule from similar examples.

Work Page . . . .

Match the Cognitive Dysfunctions

The Student Who	Is Displaying
1. continually asks what to do after the task has been explained	a. a lack of planning behavior
2. relates a story about his or her dog when the discussion is about camels	b. an impaired need for summative behavior
3. seeks confirmation that he or she has copied correctly despite having the original still in front of him or her	c. impaired elaboration of cognitive strategies
4. has difficulty "thinking out loud" and drawing abstract conclusions	d. a lack of internalization
5. has difficulty finding methods of testing assumptions	e. an inability to select relevant cues
6. will not concern him- or herself with the "how many" of things (e.g., the totality of events)	f. impaired hypothesis testing
7. is unable to apply existing rules to new situations	g. a narrow mental field
8. relies on concrete stimuli to solve problems because he or she can't do it in his or her head	h. lack of spontaneous comparative behavior
9. views objects and events as isolated, unrelated entities	i. an episodic grasp of reality
10. is satisfied with and gives "just because" answers	j. inaccurate definition of the problem
11. cannot delay gratification or invest in long-term planning	k. lack of a need for logical evidence
12. cannot predict outcomes using "If . . . , then" thinking	l. an inability to project virtual relationships
13. fails to use relevant information learned in the past to solve a problem in the present	m. restricted use of inferential-hypothetical thinking

Chapter **16**

Output

I f one were to overhear some or all of these comments about a student's thinking, then it is likely that the student is experiencing difficulty at the output phase of the thinking process.

- "Put yourself in her shoes."
- "Try to be a bit more empathic and sensitive."
- "Can you explain that a bit more clearly?"
- "Don't just give up, let's try again!"
- "Don't just randomly guess!"
- "Your statement was wrong and inaccurate."
- "I don't understand your instructions."
- "Think of a system for working out the answer."
- "Think before you shout out the answer."
- "That's a very careless answer."
- "You copied that incorrectly from the board again."
- "Imagine it in your head before you try to draw it."
- "Tearing up your exercise book won't solve the problem."

OUTPUT PHASE

Youth workers, probation officers, judges, and law officers speak in amazement of the way in which children released on bail go and commit the same offence again. It seems a sort of imbecilic madness, but in fact the children lack the cognitive apparatus to fully control their behavior. Their inability to visualize the future means they cannot learn from past experience. The impulsive "situational" character of juvenile and much adult crime has now been recognized by criminologists on both sides of the Atlantic. In the Canadian penal system, Feuerstein's program has been implemented for adult prisoners with enthusiastic reports from the prison administrators

involved. It is precisely the emphasis of the program on reducing impulsiveness, and in developing higher critical abilities for prisoners in their dealings with their environment, that has attracted them. (Sharron, 1987, p. 56)

The output phase is the third step in the thinking process. At this point, the information that was gathered in the input phase and worked on or processed in the elaboration phase is communicated as an answer, solution, or product.

The quality of certain output functions will vary with the accuracy and success of elaboration. Similarly, the kind of output response may affect future data gathering and problem solving. On the other hand, competence in input and elaboration may be marred by difficulty at the output phase.

A student with difficulties at the output phase may see things only from his or her point of view. This student may randomly guess at answers or become frustrated and give up. The student's poor expressive language may make it difficult to communicate a response, or he or she may be careless and inaccurate. The student could experience difficulty holding an image in his or her mind's eye or rush into an answer without carefully considering it first.

This chapter deals with problems at the output phase of thinking. A detailed discussion of how to identify each dysfunction is provided and suggestions are made for correcting the dysfunction using Feuerstein's criteria of mediation.

Use the following table to identify each child's cognitive dysfunction in the classroom.

Output	
Functions	**Dysfunctions**
Communication Modalities	
Mature	Egocentric
Output Responses	
Participatory	Blocking
Output Responses	
Worked Through	Trial and Error
Expressive Verbal Tools	
Adequate	Impaired
Data Output	
Precise and Accurate	Impaired
Visual Transport	
Accurate	Impaired
Behavior	
Appropriate	Impulsive or Acting Out

COMMUNICATION MODALITIES

Description

This communication deficiency refers to the way the egocentric individual perceives his partner in a given transaction. . . . In this relationship he (i.e., the student) does not feel the need to spell out in a detailed and clear way what he thinks and why, since he considers this as known to the other as it is to him. (Feuerstein, 1979, p. 68)

The student won't accept other points of view.

Mature Communication Modalities	*Egocentric Communication Modalities*
Mature communication refers to the ability to	The student who displays egocentric communication may
■ Communicate in an empathic and flexible way (i.e., to see things from others' points of view)	■ Relate to the world only from his or her own point of view (e.g., cannot accommodate opinions or approaches that differ from his or her own, shouts down others who are trying to get across a point)
■ Appreciate that others do not intuitively know what is being thought, and therefore develop the skills necessary for effective interpersonal communication and be able and willing to provide detailed, precise, and solid arguments in response to questions and tasks	■ Believe that others think the same way as he or she does, and therefore has difficulties elaborating, expanding, or giving reasons for responses
■ Listen to and take into consideration the perspective of others	■ Be insensitive to social cues and, as a result, respond inappropriately

Various Occurrences

Egocentrism occurs when a student is self-centered and fails to take into account others' points of view. When communicating, the student may ignore or even spurn the needs of others. At the input phase, there is a reluctance to consider more than one source of information. At the elaboration phase, there is little need to provide evidence for one's ideas. At the output phase, this results in communicating ideas only from one's own perspective.

Example

A student will exhibit egocentric communication by dominating a group activity and demanding that everyone does it "his or her way," but neglect to share or explain his or her methods to the group—this student acts alone. The student fails to understand why other members are experiencing difficulties.

STRATEGIES

Examples

Strategies to Correct Egocentric Communication

Meaning

The teacher encourages a more complete response.

"Now tell me exactly what you mean when you say. . . ."

☐ Do not accept incomplete responses; demand explanations to answers.

☐ Feign an inability to understand the students' responses until they are clear and unambiguous; query the responses (e.g., "Do you mean this, or that?").

☐ Establish goals for communication and show what happens when partial messages are given (e.g., play "post office").

☐ Expose students to new forms of communication (e.g., jargon or different dialects) and allow them to experience and discuss the problems associated with them.

Self-Regulation and Control of Behavior

The teacher encourages precision using self-checking.

"Check to make sure that you have given us clear and accurate directions."

☐ Insist on precision and accuracy by showing students how to think out loud when solving a problem.

☐ Foster the discipline of asking oneself why, how, and what.

☐ Encourage students to not just assume that everyone else automatically understands them but to check that their messages have been received and understood.

Sharing

The teacher promotes empathic thinking.

"What you said is valid, but let's hear other points of view."

☐ Encourage students to examine problems from various perspectives and contrast their different points of view.

☐ Give students controversial topics to debate and help them summarize the pros and cons.

☐ Allow students to role play situations that will allow them to "get into the other person's shoes."

☐ Ask students to write or speak using slang.

OUTPUT RESPONSES I

Description

Blocking may range from a lack of initiation of new responses to an open avoidance of stimuli . . . it is a response to cognitive failure which affects the readiness of the person to enter again into a situation that may lead to failure. (Feuerstein et al., 1986, 3.17)

The student's blocking response results in his reluctance to even try.

Participatory Output Responses I

Participatory output responses refers to the ability to

- Try again, despite previous failure.
- Persevere with difficult or unfamiliar tasks.
- Initiate a different approach or strategy when a previous method was unsuccessful.
- Show an interest in solving new problems.
- Develop a sense of positive self-concept and confidence when confronting a task or activity that is more challenging.

Blocking Output Responses I

The student who experiences blocking output responses could exhibit:

- A lack of confidence when presented with challenges
- Poor motivation to attempt a new or difficult task
- Lack of perseverance to complete a task (e.g., gives up easily and quickly)
- A reluctance to try again or to try a different way when unsuccessful at a task
- Emotional outbursts (e.g., tear up his or her work book, run away, refuse to answer, cry)

Various Occurrences

Clear, systematic, and precise data gathering at the input phase will result in an accurate definition of the problem at the elaboration phase. Confidence in understanding what is required in a task will lead to an efficient problem-solving approach. Motivation to solve the task will ensure participatory output responses and help to overcome any blocking.

Example

A student who has already failed at a task is unwilling to try again because of fears of repeated failure. This results in a poor self-concept and lack of confidence in his or her ability to succeed. The student would rather run away than once again face failure, embarrassment, and/or frustration.

STRATEGIES

Examples	**Strategies to Correct Blocking**

Intentionality and Reciprocity

The teacher invites participation by simplifying a difficult problem.

"Don't give up. Let's break up this problem into parts and solve it step by step."

☐ Remove any ambiguous or confusing examples that might cause concern.

☐ Present tasks that focus on the students' likes and interests, which will arouse curiosity and stimulate them to participate and become involved.

☐ Anticipate and intervene in areas of potential difficulty (e.g., break up a difficult task into small parts or suggest a different approach).

Competence

The teacher helps to motivate students by reducing their fear of failure.

"Examining mistakes can be valuable because it shows us where we went wrong."

☐ Suggest problem-solving approaches that are within the students' level of competence (work from strength to weakness), focusing on the positive responses.

☐ Reward and give credit for attempting a new task and persevering with a difficult one.

☐ Allay anxiety by reassuring the students that they can produce a valuable response.

☐ Show that there are no negative consequences to producing a wrong answer (i.e., we learn from our mistakes).

Self-Regulation and Control of Behavior

The teacher tries to break the self-defeating habit of blocking.

"Instead of saying 'I can't,' let's say 'I'll try.'"

☐ Replace the students' habit of avoiding a difficult task by motivating them to try.

☐ Model the process of problem solving by talking out loud when solving a task.

☐ When working with students, provide them with encouragement and the skills to succeed.

☐ Show the students how to check their work regularly so they can monitor their progress.

☐ Encourage the students to evaluate their behavior in terms of positive achievements rather than focusing on failures.

OUTPUT RESPONSES II

Description

Trial-and-error learning may actually reinforce a kind of probabilistic, random behavior, diverting the attention of the individual and distracting him from the relationships to be discovered. (Feuerstein, 1980, p. 100)

I'll do this first. No ... this? Um ... I'll just have to guess.

The student's random trial-and-error responses reflect an unstructured approach.

Worked Through Output Responses II

A student who gives a worked-through response is able to

- Solve and communicate problems systematically
- Work logically and rationally through a problem
- Impose order onto what may at first seem like a bombardment of bits of information
- Establish a goal and devise a strategy to reach it

Trial and Error Output Responses II

The student who gives trial-and-error responses may

- Randomly and impulsively guess at answers
- Not think ahead or plan a strategy
- Tend to repeat errors and not learn from mistakes
- Learn little from unstructured learning environments
- Have difficulties with defining and keeping his or her goal in mind, or may change strategies repeatedly
- Communicate data in a random, unplanned manner until by chance he or she finds a solution

---

Various Occurrences

The possibility of a worked-through response begins at the input phase, at which careful exploration of the learning situation is necessary. Working through a problem at the elaboration phase means that the necessary cognitive functions are applied in defining it and finding its solution. At the output phase, impulsivity is controlled and responses are communicated in a planned and systematic manner.

Example

Trial-and-error behavior or "discovery learning" is an acceptable problem-solving strategy for efficient students. However, the student who has an episodic grasp of reality cannot benefit from random and arbitrary learning because he or she does not possess the thinking skills to interpret the data. If the student cannot draw conclusions, infer patterns, and learn from mistakes, then errors will follow more errors until a structure is mediated

STRATEGIES

Examples

Strategies to Correct Trial-and-Error Responses

Meaning

The teacher models systematic thinking.

"First, let me work out a plan for this job; then. . . ."

- ☐ Model how a systematic approach to tasks results in success (e.g., in making a cake, conducting an experiment, doing a puzzle or a math problem, sorting, finding lost objects).
- ☐ Show how "worked-through" responses are more likely to lead to success as inferior responses will have been discarded along the way (e.g., solving a math problem using logical calculation rather than guess work).
- ☐ Demonstrate how using proper investigational strategies to solve a problem can be as important as the answer because the strategies can be used again in different situations.

Self-Regulation and Control of Behavior

The teacher encourages self-regulation by asking students to create their own mottos.

"'Engage brain before putting mouth into gear.'"

- ☐ Have students make up mottos in order to monitor their behavior and control random and impulsive responses (e.g., "Think before you ink!").
- ☐ Develop a strategy by asking questions like *"What* must I do? *How* will I do it? *How* can I check it?"
- ☐ Encourage students to reflect on the inefficiency of trial-and-error responses and to self-correct.
- ☐ Show students how to critically evaluate arguments and modify them accordingly.

Competence

The teacher rewards a systematic approach to a task.

"See how your strategy helped you. Well done!"

- ☐ Praise the development of a strategy in approaching a task, even if the answer is wrong.
- ☐ Take time to identify specific difficulties of students and give individual help.
- ☐ Focus on concrete, task-oriented responses; move toward more abstract strategies once a systematic approach has been established.

EXPRESSIVE VERBAL TOOLS

Description

At the output phase the existence of verbal codes permits the use of more complex relationships and facilitates the understanding and communication of more abstract operations and relations. (Feuerstein et al., 1986, 3.7)

The student has difficulty with everyday language.

Adequate Expressive Verbal Tools

Adequate expressive verbal tools refers to the ability to

- Verbally communicate a response that can be understood

- Use expressive language (e.g., having the words to say what you mean, finding the labels to describe processes, and selecting the correct words to give clear and precise descriptions)

- Select the appropriate word(s) from long-term memory to communicate answers clearly and effectively

Impaired Expressive Verbal Tools

The student who manifests impaired expressive verbal tools may

- Have poor communication skills (e.g., use gestures rather than words)

- Exhibit poor knowledge and use of vocabulary, grammar, and sentence structures (syntax)

- Be inflexible, lack creativity, and experience difficulties in selecting appropriate words, phrases, clauses, and sentences

- Show poor verbal fluency and inadequate recall of words, phrases, and sentences from long-term memory (this could result in repetition, prolonged pauses, using imprecise words, word-finding difficulties, circumlocution, overuse of words, etc.)

- Find the solutions to problems but be unable to explain to others how he or she will achieve this

Various Occurrences

The absence of specific verbal labels at the input phase will result in the inability to think about and solve tasks in the elaboration phase. At the output phase, inadequate verbal expression hampers communication of ideas, answers, and solutions.

Example

In the classroom, the student may be unable to ask and answer questions effectively. This could result in difficulties expressing ideas clearly and concisely, giving directions, following instructions, or summarizing information. In English class, the student will struggle to express his or her point of view and have difficulty using creative and descriptive language.

STRATEGIES

Examples

Strategies to Correct Impaired Expressive Verbal Tools

Competence

The teacher extends vocabulary.

"How many words can you think of to describe the animal in this picture."

☐ Encourage spontaneous discussion of a variety of topics to build confidence.

☐ Determine the students' competence in the language of instruction in order to formulate a vocabulary enrichment program.

Meaning

The teacher encourages accurate language use.

"The word 'infuriate' has been used incorrectly here. Rephrase your sentence so it makes sense."

☐ Encourage students to generate a number of alternative words and praise them for selecting the most accurate or descriptive ones.

☐ Encourage students to use self-talk as a strategy for building confidence in conversation.

☐ Determine whether a difficulty is limited to the oral or written modality and provide opportunities for using both.

☐ Encourage meaningful use of language by discussing film, drama, or pictures.

☐ Provide exercises to practice accurate language use (e.g., sentence completion and filling in the blank).

☐ Develop the use of figurative and creative language by helping students elaborate on ideas and describe stories in detail.

☐ Provide opportunities for structural analysis or decoding of words in order to facilitate a better understanding of language.

Sense of Belonging

The teacher encourages the labeling and explanation of relationships.

"Your mother's father's father would be your Great Grandfather on your mother's side."

☐ Provide practice in expressing relationships clearly and concisely in everyday life by
  - Attaching the correct labels to family members (e.g., great aunt, grandmother, niece, second cousin)
  - Researching words for these relationships in other cultures (e.g., Buba, nana, auntie)
  - Allowing students to share their family trees with the class
  - Encouraging individuals to talk about their culture and language with other students

☐ Encourage students to relay and interpret their family experiences using their own words, ideas, role plays, etc.

DATA OUTPUT

Description

We conceive the need for precision and accuracy to be the result of an interactive process between the individual and his environment, and to reflect an attitudinal and stylistic approach to life. (Feuerstein et al., 1986, p. 67)

The student's response is characterized by careless errors.

Precise and Accurate Data Output

Precise and accurate data output refers to the ability to

- Communicate a response that is detailed and correct
- Transmit data efficiently without omissions and distortions of collected information
- Produce answers that show careful consideration and selective use of collected material
- Internalize a need to collect and present information that is specific and appropriate
- Develop a habit for presenting information in a clear and relevant way
- Explain facts in absolute rather than relative terms and to quantify rather than use approximations

Impaired Data Output

The student who shows impaired data output may

- Communicate data inaccurately or incompletely, omitting or distorting collected facts and details
- Present responses that are narrow, one-sided, unclear, or vague
- Present material in a meaningless way because cognitive skills such as comparison and summation have been ineffective at the elaboration phase
- Show trial-and-error responses, rushed and premature (impulsive) responses, and poor use of language with the result that data are produced inaccurately and imprecisely
- Give attention to irrelevant and inappropriate information in response to a question

---

Various Occurrences

At the input phase, precision and accuracy are established by gathering information clearly and systematically. This ensures that problem solving at the elaboration phase occurs without serious errors. At the output phase, responses will be communicated effectively and precisely

Example

The student has not developed the desire or need to work out a problem systematically and thoroughly. His or her work is continually marred by careless errors and inadequate detail. The student's math problems may reflect numbers that have been left out (inaccurate) or his or her English essay may be vague and confusing (imprecise).

STRATEGIES

Examples	Strategies to Correct Impaired Data Output

Meaning

The teacher points out the value of precision.

"Joe's answer was excellent because he read the instructions carefully."

☐ Show how imprecise data gathering will distort communication and result in erroneous answers.

☐ Give feedback on gaps in knowledge produced by imprecision, and show how this results in a poor understanding of the subject under discussion.

☐ Promote study skills to improve accurate communication of gathered information (e.g., looking for main ideas, summarizing key words, detailing important facts).

Transcendence

The teacher insists on accuracy when giving information.

"Sue, give us the exact details of the itinerary for our Washington, D.C., field trip."

☐ Encourage students to focus on details when describing experiences they see, hear, or touch.

☐ Allow students to role play and present reports of daily events (e.g., a newspaper reporter, detective, TV personality, sports commentator, travel guide).

☐ Analyze political speeches, newspaper bias, etc., in terms of precise and accurate delivery.

Self-Regulation and Control of Behavior

The teacher encourages self-correction.

"This essay is confusing. Try to rewrite it so that each paragraph deals with a new idea."

☐ Encourage students to give clear instructions to others and allow them to act out how imprecise communication can cause misunderstandings.

☐ Guide students' answers by providing explicit step-by-step instructions.

☐ Gradually reduce dependency on the mediator by encouraging the students' need for establishing their own guidelines for precision.

☐ Deliberately present information such as a report or a story imprecisely, or in an absurd manner, and ask the students to pinpoint errors in the presentation.

☐ Encourage students to rework essays before handing them in.

☐ Allow students to "be the teacher" and correct their own work in order to learn from their evaluations.

VISUAL TRANSPORT

Description

Deficiency of visual transport is defined as the incapacity of the retarded performer to complete a given figure by visually transporting a missing part from a number of alternatives. (Feuerstein, 1980, p. 101)

The student has difficulty transferring visual images.

Accurate Visual Transport

Accurate visual transport refers to the ability to

- Perceive and then memorize visual details clearly
- Refer to a familiar and well-established concept in order to accurately identify or reproduce it without distortions (e.g., understanding the difference between a square and a rectangle in order to reproduce the square)
- Carry an image in one's mind and move it from one place to another (e.g., fitting a circle into various frames/backgrounds)
- Mentally manipulate visual detail in order to internally reorient the image (e.g., rotating a puzzle piece until it fits)

Impaired Visual Transport

Impaired visual transport could be indicated by the following

- A poor understanding of concepts (e.g., drawing a triangle when the model is a square)
- An immature reference system (e.g., inability to describe left, right, top, bottom)
- Incorrect or inaccurate reproductions of original stimuli (e.g., leaving out details when copying a picture)
- An inability to focus on relevant or sufficient detail (visual cues) (e.g., misspelling a word when copying it from the board)
- Poor visual memory or recall (e.g., inability to remember how to form a letter or draw a picture from memory)

Various Occurrences

At the input phase, visual information should be clearly perceived. At the elaboration phase, this information is mentally manipulated in order to reproduce it at the output phase. This reproduction should be transported to an area different than the one in which it was originally perceived.

Example

A student with impaired visual transport may reproduce a parallelogram as a rectangle or the number 2 may be inverted to 5. In this case, the visual information has been incorrectly reproduced. The student may also have difficulty revisualizing a stimulus without it being there (e.g., drawing a picture of a house from memory or putting together the pieces of a puzzle).

STRATEGIES

Examples

Strategies to Correct Impaired Visual Transport

Intentionality and Reciprocity

The teacher encourages a careful and controlled focus on stimuli.

"Take the time to look carefully and describe it in detail before you copy it."

☐ Use the verbal modality to help the visual (e.g., describe and label the figure that is being copied [visually transported]).

☐ Encourage the students to focus attention on specific details of the stimuli by highlighting certain areas (e.g., color code, enlarge, underline).

☐ Focus on the visual stimuli for an extended period of time, which allows for clear and systematic data gathering.

☐ Show students techniques they can use to recall visual data (e.g., tracing patterns on the board with their eyes or fingers).

Self-Regulation and Control of Behavior

The teacher suggests a strategy for accurate copying.

"Let's see if we have copied it correctly by checking from left to right."

☐ Encourage students to revisualize an image before making a physical representation (e.g., "Picture it in your head before you draw it.").

☐ Control impulsivity by encouraging students to explain the task in their own words.

☐ Emphasize the importance of transporting visual information in the correct sequence (e.g., words are letters in a specific sequence or order).

☐ Develop the need to check the original model to assess the accuracy of the visual transfer.

☐ Encourage the students to work in pairs, checking each other's work, and explaining any errors when copying.

Sharing

The teacher encourages analysis when copying to ensure accuracy.

"All the words should end in -ing."

☐ Help students make meaning of visual stimuli by breaking them down into parts (e.g., prefix and suffix, root words, finding a square in a complex figure).

☐ Establish a reference system to enable students to position visual images correctly in space (e.g., meaningful use of prepositions; understanding of left, right, top, bottom).

☐ Encourage students to reread copied information to ensure that it has meaning.

BEHAVIOR

Description

Impulsivity may be manifest at the output phase. One common phenomenon is the absurd, and totally unexpected, erroneous answers offered by children. (Feuerstein, 1980, p. 80)

The student who responds prematurely will miss essential details.

Appropriate Behavior

Appropriate output behavior refers to the ability to

- Delay a response until all information has been systematically processed (i.e., "just a moment let me think")
- Balance the desire to complete a task rapidly with the need to invest appropriate attention to complete the task accurately (i.e., the correct answer is better than a fast answer)
- Use proper investigational strategies to formulate an accurate response
- Work through all incoming information (tactile or auditory) carefully and systematically in order to arrive at an appropriate answer

Impulsive/Acting Out Behavior

The student who manifests impulsive/acting-out behavior may

- Act inappropriately (e.g., clown around, shout out, have difficulty taking turns and containing responses)
- Give careless answers without sufficient attention to details
- Arrive at wrong answers without taking the time to gather data properly and plan answers
- Give the right answer in one modality but not in another (e.g., a correct verbal but incorrect written response)
- Say the first thing that comes to mind in order to impress his or her peers or teacher with a quick and snappy answer

---

Various Occurrences

Unplanned and hasty exploration of a learning situation will impact all three phases of thinking. At the input phase, it will manifest itself in an unsympathetic approach to a problem. At the elaboration phase, it will result in an inability to think systematically through the problem. At the output phase, it may result in a rushed, premature, or incorrect response.

Example

In the classroom, the student will attend to the first and most salient stimulus before he or she has had an opportunity to gather all the data available. This will result in absurd and often totally unexpected erroneous answers in various areas of functioning (e.g., in an exam or test, anxiety might cause the student to rush into a response without careful consideration).

STRATEGIES

Examples

Strategies to Correct Impulsive or Acting-Out Behavior

Self-Regulation and Control of Behavior

The teacher encourages self-control.

"Come up with your own motto to remind you to 'think before you ink.'"

☐ Discourage quick and snappy answers.

☐ After posing a question, allow students sufficient time to formulate a response.

☐ Encourage students to monitor their own behavior in order to delay responses and develop self-discipline.

☐ Develop a need to plan ahead and assess data before taking action.

☐ Discuss strategies for inhibiting impulsivity (e.g., restrain outbursts by counting to ten first, draw a mind map before writing an essay).

Meaning

The teacher provides a reason for control.

"Consider all aspects; otherwise your conclusions will be incomplete."

☐ Ask students to think about the why and the how of acting appropriately in different situations (e.g., playground behavior is different than classroom behavior).

☐ Explain that a hasty approach may have dangerous consequences (e.g., rushing across a road).

☐ Encourage students to include all relevant data in their responses by listing, comparing, summarizing, etc.

☐ Emphasize the importance of the means (e.g., rough drafts or the approach taken) rather than the end (e.g., answers or products).

Competence

The teacher praises reflective thinking.

"Well done! You thought that through before responding."

☐ Allow the students to initially express themselves in the modality they are most comfortable and least impulsive with (e.g., spoken before written response).

☐ Acknowledge the students' improvements in attempting to control inappropriate behavior.

☐ Reward students for waiting for their turn before responding.

☐ Provide the students with tools and strategies that can be used to improve their responses (e.g., listening skills, role playing).

Work Page ·

Identify the Following Output Dysfunctions

1. Difficulty with expressive language.

   _____

2. Tendency to randomly guess at answers.

   _____

3. Inaccurate or incomplete response to problems.

   _____

4. Inability to memorize visual details in order to reproduce them at a later stage.

   _____

5. Uncontrolled, inappropriate responses.

   _____

6. Inability to differentiate or see things from another perspective.

   _____

7. Lack of initiation of new responses and an open avoidance of stimuli.

   _____

Work Page ·

Match the Cognitive Dysfunctions

The Student Who	*Is Displaying*
1. makes "silly" mistakes (e.g., adds instead of subtracts)	a. impulsive output behavior
2. cannot respond empathically or see things from another's point of view	b. blocking behavior
3. has difficulty planning ahead and working systematically	c. egocentric communication
4. draws a triangle from the model, which is a square	d. imprecision in data output
5. has difficulty explaining his or her answers	e. trial-and-error responses
6. tears up his or her answer sheet	f. impaired visual transport
7. rushes through his or her responses without checking	g. impaired expressive verbal tools

PART IV

Metatask

The Cognitive Map

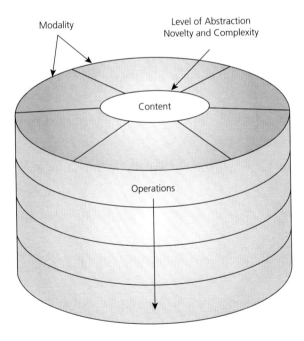

- How can the learning experience be modified?

- What are the thinking skills needed to solve the task?

- How is the task presented? Can the subject matter be varied?

- Is the task concrete or abstract?

- How unusual or difficult is the task?

Part IV attempts to answer these questions by discussing Feuerstein's model of the Cognitive Map.

Chapter 17

Analyzing the Task

This final part outlines the map or tool that Feuerstein has developed to construct and analyze a teaching task. This map shows how a teacher or caregiver might vary or change a learning experience to identify why and where a learner is having cognitive difficulties. The Cognitive Map can be used as a tool for analyzing and manipulating a teaching experience to identify cognitive dysfunctions and improve thinking, enabling us to focus on the task and engage in metatask thinking. It enables us to answer the question:

How can the learning task be analyzed to identify and develop efficient thinking skills?

The Cognitive Map consists of four layers of analysis that can be unpacked to focus on specific aspects of the task. Each layer provides a different area of analysis and opportunity for interaction. These four layers focus on

1. The content or subject matter of the task

2. The modality or language of presentation of the task

3. The level of abstraction, novelty, and complexity of the task

4. The cognitive operation or thinking skills required by the task

Each layer is analyzed and varied in isolation and then the whole is put back together. This analysis and synthesis of the task allows for multiple variations, which offers the mediator multiple ways to approach a learning experience. As the name suggests, the Cognitive Map offers a map whereby the teacher can navigate the learning situation to re-mediate cognitive functions.

> *This conceptual model is not a map in the topographical sense but a tool by which to locate specific problem areas and to produce changes in corresponding dimensions.*
>
> —Feuerstein et al., 1986, p. 1.4

CONTENT

The first layer of analysis of the Cognitive Map is the universe of content around which the mental act is centered. The questions that the mediator needs to ask when analyzing the content include

- What is the content or subject matter?
- Is the subject matter familiar to the learner?
- Can the subject matter be varied to aid cognitive development?

The success of engaging with a task is dependent on whether the learner is familiar and comfortable with the content. This depends on the learner's background, schooling, culture, and past experiences. If learners are unfamiliar or uncomfortable with the content, this will interfere with their ability to engage with problem solving. The emphasis will shift to trying to make sense of the content rather than solving the underlying cognitive challenge.

Content

Consider the following example:

An English teacher in a poetry class is concerned that the students are having difficulty with the cognitive skill of imagery—in particular simile and metaphor. The poem the class is studying uses the metaphor of a swan. The teacher asks the students to put up their hands if they know what a swan is or have ever seen a swan. No hands are raised. The class consists of a group of children living in a low socio-economic inner-city area that have not been exposed to lakes, parks, or zoos where they might have seen a swan. It thus emerges that it is not the cognitive skill of imagery (simile and metaphor) that is problematic—it is rather the content or subject matter of "swan" that is totally foreign to the learner. The teacher then uses images of buildings and traffic and crowded streets and the students have no difficulty understanding and generating their own similes and metaphors. Hence the environment, background, and culture of these learners determines which content is more familiar, and this influences their thinking.

The questions about content of the above task that can be used within the Cognitive Map include the following:

What is the content/subject matter of the task?

Answer: The content of the poem involves imagery about swans.

Is the subject matter familiar to the learner?

Answer: No—inner-city students were unfamiliar with wild swans.

Can the subject matter be varied to aid cognitive development of the task?

Answer: Yes—familiar content (e.g., busy street images) can be used to teach the concept of simile and metaphor, or the learner can be exposed to the content of swans through pictures, images, an outing to the zoo, etc.

MODALITY

The second layer of analysis of the Cognitive Map is the modality, or language in which the content is expressed. The modality of a task could be verbal, pictorial, numerical, figural, symbolic, graphic, or a combination of these. The modality influences learning to the extent that we have preferred modalities when problem solving. Some learners are more visual thinkers, while others prefer the verbal modality. Content in different modalities can yield different responses. The questions that the mediator needs to ask when analyzing the modality or language include

- How is the task presented? Is it written, verbal, pictorial, etc.?
- Can the mode of presentation be varied?

It is not reliable to diagnose a cognitive difficulty unless a number of different modalities have been used in mediation.

Modality

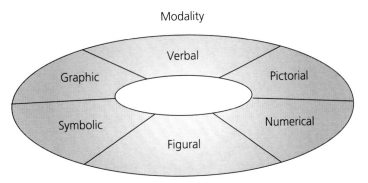

Consider the following example:

A mother gives her son some money to go to the corner shop and buy three lollipops for his younger siblings. She asks how much change he should receive. The child has difficulty mentally calculating the mathematical operation when it is presented verbally. Presented in this modality, the child has to convert the story sum into numbers, solve the numerical exercise mentally, and then respond verbally. He is unable to do this as a mental computation; however, when given a pen and paper, the child is able to write down the numbers into a multiplication sum and quickly solve it. It is the verbal modality that presents the difficulty, not an inability to solve a cognitive mathematical task. It is thus unreliable to suggest there is a difficulty understanding mathematical reasoning when only one modality to assess this is presented.

> The questions about the modality of the above task include the following:
>
> How is the task presented? Is it written, verbal, pictoral, etc.?
> *Answer:* The mathematical reasoning problem was presented orally as a story sum.
>
> Can the mode of presentation be varied?
> *Answer:* Yes, the modality can be changed to be numerical (using numbers) in a written form (pen and paper).

LEVELS OF ABSTRACTION, NOVELTY, AND COMPLEXITY

The third layer of analysis of the Cognitive Map is the level of abstraction, novelty, and complexity of the task. These relate to whether the task is concrete (hands-on), whether it is familiar to the learner, and how difficult it is. The questions that the mediator needs to ask when analyzing the level of abstraction, novelty, and complexity include

- Can the task be presented in a way that moves from concrete to abstract?
- Can the learner be given practice so the task becomes more familiar?
- Can an easier example of the task be introduced initially and then graded in difficulty?

In all tasks a learner should be given opportunities to move from the concrete to the abstract, from the familiar to the novel, and from easy to complex.

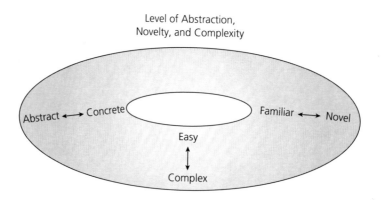

Consider the following example:

A child is having difficulty with the cognitive operation of synthesis in piecing together a jigsaw puzzle. There are a number of different elements within this task that can be manipulated to teach this skill of synthesis. The first is the level of abstraction. If the child is required to put the jigsaw together just by looking at the separate pieces, it is a highly abstract task. This would involve making sense of each separate part and then integrating the pieces into a mental hypothetical (abstract) whole. This can be made more concrete by giving the child an actual picture of the finished jigsaw to work toward. Thus the child will be working from the concrete picture to piece together an abstract integrated whole.

The level of novelty of the task is the second area to consider when mediating the jigsaw puzzle task. If this is the first time the child has been confronted with solving a puzzle, it will be very unfamiliar, and there will be cognitive overload working out first what to do and then how to do it. The mediator can demonstrate putting another jigsaw puzzle together, thus modeling the skill of synthesizing parts into a whole. The mediator can work with the learner on a few more puzzles, scaffolding the process and gradually withdrawing support. The more familiar the task, the more competent the learner will become.

Level of complexity is the third area to consider when mediating the jigsaw puzzle. Jigsaw puzzles range in difficulty—from number of puzzle pieces to complexity of design to 3D models. The mediator can start teaching synthesis by working on a simple picture with a few pieces. Gradually the difficulty level can be increased as the learner begins to consider all the variables when solving a puzzle—such as identifying and considering color, shape, and size all simultaneously. As the learner becomes competent in the skills of synthesis, the level of complexity can increase.

The questions about the level of abstraction, novelty, and complexity of the above task include the following:

Can the task be presented in a concrete way?

Answer: Yes, providing a concrete picture of the overall jigsaw puzzle will give a structure to work toward in mentally interpreting how each piece fits together into a whole.

Can the learner be given practice so the task becomes more familiar?

Answer: Yes, modeling how and what to do and working initially with the learner helps to scaffold the learning experience.

Can an easier example of the task be introduced initially?

Answer: Yes, decreasing the level of difficulty enables the learner to become competent at the task before more complex elements and examples are given.

COGNITIVE OPERATION

The final layer of analysis of the Cognitive Map is the cognitive operations or thinking skills which the task demands. Solving any mental activity requires a range of thinking skills from the most simple level (e.g., identifying the problem, comparing the items) to very complex thinking skills (e.g., inductive reasoning, transitive thinking). The layers of cognitive operations of any task need to be analyzed to be able to pinpoint specific difficulty and mediate effectively. The questions that the mediator needs to ask when analyzing the cognitive operations include

- What are the thinking skills involved in solving this task?
- How can these thinking skills be mediated?

It is not reliable to diagnose an overall difficulty with a cognitive operation unless the underlying cognitive skills that make up that operation have been mediated.

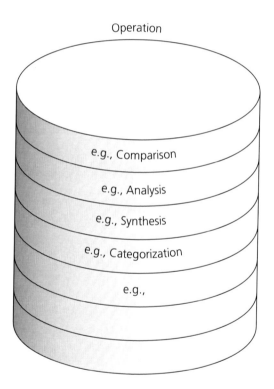

Operation

e.g., Comparison

e.g., Analysis

e.g., Synthesis

e.g., Categorization

e.g.,

Consider the following example:

A career counselor is working with a class to help them decide their future career direction. This is a complex decision-making exercise and requires the class to engage in a number of different thinking skills. The most elementary of these is to identify and describe a range of career options. Once students have mastered the skills of identifying and describing they then have to be able to compare. The cognitive skill of comparison involves selecting relevant and appropriate criteria by which to compare. In terms of career choice, relevant criteria for selecting careers might include issues like values, life-style, interests, and skills. Students will need to be able to identify their own values, skills, and interests and match these to the various career options. Different careers can then be compared based on lifestyles, job opportunities, salaries, etc. Each one of these operations or skills such as identification, description, and comparison can be mediated in order to build up to the complex skill of evaluation and decision making.

The questions about the operation that can be used to teach the thinking skills required in the task include

What are the thinking skills involved in solving this task?

Answer: Identification, description, comparison, and evaluation are all needed in making decisions about a career choice.

How can these thinking skills be mediated?

Answer: Identification and description requires attention to detail and research skills.
Comparison involves looking at similarities and differences.
Evaluation requires logical judgment based on appropriate and relevant criteria.
As outlined above, the Cognitive Map enables the mediator to manipulate the task in order to identify difficulty and teach the necessary cognitive skills.

Feuerstein's Instrumental Enrichment (IE) program is designed, using the Cognitive Map, to teach the following thinking skills:

- Organization
- Comparison
- Orientation in space
- Analytic perception
- Categorization
- Temporal relations
- Following instructions
- Numerical progressions
- Transitive relations
- Syllogisms

These can be bridged into the classroom, home, and counseling context (see our *Bridging Learning, In and Out of the Classroom Manual*, 1999).

Work Page ....

In the example presented below, use the Cognitive Map to analyze and modify the task.

Example: Word Categories Task

Sort the following word list into four different categories and give a concept for each category. Use the table below.

Basil, orange, custard, carrot, celery, parsley, apple, apricot, fennel, grape, mint, yogurt, cream, lettuce, potato, milk

_____	_____	_____	_____

Analysis According to the Cognitive Map

Task: Word Categories

Content

1. What is the content/subject matter?

_____

2. Can the subject matter be varied to aid cognitive development?

_____

Modality

1. How is the task presented? Is it written, verbal, pictorial, etc.?

_____

2. Can the mode of presentation be varied?

_____

Levels of Abstraction, Novelty, and Complexity

1. Can the task be presented in a way that moves from concrete to abstract?

_____

2. Can the learner be given practice so the task becomes more familiar?

_____

3. Can an easier example of the task be introduced initially?

_____

Cognitive Operation

1. What are the thinking skills involved in solving this task?

_____

2. How can these thinking skills be mediated?

_____

Resource A

Answers to Work Pages

PART II. METATEACHING: MEDIATED LEARNING EXPERIENCE

Intentionality and Reciprocity (Pages 19–20)

Case Study

1. The teacher did not motivate the student and hence did not mediate intentionality effectively.

2. None, Sipho is confused and overwhelmed and is not responding to the initiated activity.

3. The teacher could capture attention by providing/eliciting examples and asking students whether they understand the exercise or if they need any assistance.

True or False

1. True

2. False. It may result in intentionality, but merely coming to class prepared does not ensure that intentionality will occur.

Define

Mediation of intentionality and reciprocity is a mutual interaction. The mediator has the intention to share. The learner wants to receive.

Modify

Any statement that encourages more interaction, explanation, and interpretation of what to do (e.g., "Take out your English grammar books and turn to Chapter 10. Let's quickly recap what's happened so we can pick up from where we left off.").

Meaning (Pages 27–28)

Case Study

1. The father's statement fails to explain the relevance of school to Alex's future.

2. The father could have mediated meaning more effectively by explaining how school teaches life skills that are important for any career.

3. Yes. Lack of communication exists because of the breakdown of intentionality and reciprocity. Alex and his father could have discussed the issue further rather than withdrawing into themselves.

True or False

1. True

2. True. S-H-O-H-R will aid S-O-R. (See page 10)

Define

Mediation of meaning means enthusiastically sharing your aims. It answers the learner's questions about why an activity is important.

Modify

Any statement that gives a reason or value for not bullying (e.g., "Bullying is socially unacceptable and results in unpleasant consequences.") teaches life skills that are important for any career.

Transcendence (Pages 35–36)

Case Study

1. The counselor bridges Kylie's experiences in the counseling session by asking her to try out the strategies at home.

2. One of the key objectives in counseling is to ensure behaviors and cognitions are transferred to the outside world. The counselor has now empowered Kylie to try out her ideas in a different environment.

3. The counselor could link Kylie's feelings to situations in her past in which she overcame obstacles, or bridge to case histories of how different people have won in the face of adversity.

True or False

1. True

2. True

Define

Transcendence is bridging from an immediate experience to underlying principles and related activities.

Modify

Any statement that links the study of history to broader "life" goals (e.g., "The past helps us understand the present," or "We can learn to appreciate bias and different perspectives about past events.").

Competence (Pages 43–44)

Case Study

1. The teacher undermines Juanita's sense of competence by neither giving reasons for her failure nor providing guidelines for her to reach or achieve her potential.

2. Juanita has internalized the negative label and is living down to low expectations of herself—the self-fulfilling prophecy.

3. The teacher could have prefaced with a positive statement—"you have tried hard and I am pleased you attempted the test. Now we can work on improving your score. I know you are capable!"

True or False

1. False. Competence means focusing on the positive, not the negative.

2. True

Define

Mediation of competence means instilling in the learner a positive belief in his or her ability to succeed.

Modify

Any statement that rephrases the comment in a positive way (e.g., "Well done, you've made real progress—but the topic is difficult, so keep practicing.").

Self-Regulation and Control of Behavior (Pages 51–52)

Case Study

1. Yes, the mother has been active in understanding Shimon's dilemma and helped provide strategies for organization and control.

2. Shimon's reaction shows a lack of control of the situation and an inability to self-regulate.

3. The mother could work through various topics with Shimon and show him examples of how he could manage his studying with self-regulatory behaviors (e.g., keeping a study diary).

True or False

1. False. The therapist is monitoring the client's behavior and not mediating self-regulation. The therapist is doing it for the client, rendering the client dependent on him or her.

2. True. Self-checking.

Define

Self-regulation and control of behavior involves "thinking about your own thinking" and modifying your responses.

Modify

Any statement that helps the student identify his or her errors and see them as a source of learning (e.g., "See if you can find your mistakes; that'll help you learn where and why you went wrong.").

Sharing (Pages 59–60)

Case Study

1. Raj has taken it upon himself to complete the group model alone.

2. Thandi's response illustrates to Raj that his actions were not acceptable—that sharing should have occurred.

3. Teachers can organize the activities/content of group projects so that there is collaboration and task sharing (e.g., group report backs, shared presentations).

True or False

1. False. The mother who helps her child put away toys is mediating sharing (e.g., "Two hands are better than one;" "If you help me, it'll go quicker;" "I'll help you put away your toys just as you helped me put away the groceries.").

2. True

Define

Sharing promotes sensitivity toward others and emphasizes working together.

Modify

Any statement that encourages the student to share ideas, ask for help, or cooperate with others (e.g., "There are lots of sources of information for your project. Ask the librarian or your teacher, or run your ideas by your parents or friends. Talk about your project with others and it'll become clearer, and you'll get some new, good ideas.").

Individuation (Pages 67–68)

Case Study

1. Your own example.

2. The teacher's comments illustrate that she accepts and encourages Taiko's unique personality and ability; by respecting this right to be different, she mediates individuation.

3. Taiko is hesitant—perhaps he is the product of a cultural/academic system that stifles individual expression.

True or False

1. True

2. False. Simply agreeing with someone because she or he is in authority does not allow you as an individual to think for yourself.

Define

Individuation is the acknowledgment and appreciation of uniqueness and independence.

Modify

Any statement that allows the child to follow a career of his or her own choice, related to his or her own strengths and weaknesses (e.g., "Let's look at your strengths, interests, and values to help you decide on a career choice."). Parents should not be prescriptive or use emotional blackmail.

Goal Planning (Pages 75–76)

Case Study

1. There is no evidence of either-let alone planning for achieving an outcome.

2. Pedro's strengths, weaknesses, abilities, and difficulties need to be taken into account. Then Pedro's father could help Pedro set a realistic target for himself—"I will work at the car wash and in six weeks I will have enough for a new board."

3. Parents and teachers can help the individuals identify their goals and then mediate strategies that will help them reach their targets. This not only empowers the individual, but also encourages a more positive and resourceful attitude.

True or False

1. True. If you can't think in terms of the future and how the present affects the future, then you will have trouble planning long-term goals.

2. False. Goals can be reached irrespective of a change in the plan or the process of getting there. In fact, the plan or strategy to reach a goal often must be altered as obstacles are encountered.

Define

Goal planning is the process by which the student is guided to plan for and achieve goals.

Modify

Any statement that would allow the student to formulate his or her long-term goal and establish the steps needed to reach that goal (e.g., "You seem to have strengths in the mechanical area. If you want to follow a career in that direction, what steps will you have to take?").

Challenge (Pages 83–84)

Case Study

1. Yes. Sulamen mediates challenge and Mia responds negatively.

2. Mia's response indicates that she does not have enough self-confidence to rise to a challenge. She has limited belief in her talent.

3. Sulamen could motivate her by showing enthusiasm and helping her anticipate success. He could offer to help her promote herself because he believes in her talent.

True or False

1. False. Challenge complements mediation of meaning. "Culture" is not static, and while mediation of meaning transmits dominant cultural norms, a challenge of those traditions is central to MLE.

2. True. Difficult tasks can be simplified by breaking them up into smaller, easier steps.

Define

Challenge is the feeling of excitement when confronting a new and difficult task.

Modify

Any statement that would encourage students to try new and alternative methods when confronting difficult tasks (e.g., "It will be exciting to try a new approach to this difficult task and see how well we do.").

Self-Change (Pages 91–92)

Case Study

1. Hans's reflection indicates that he is developing an awareness of self-change and is taking responsibility for monitoring his own growth and change in attitude and behavior.

2. The counselor recounts events of past negative behaviors, thus helping Hans to develop an orientation to time and encouraging an expectation and acceptance of maturation and growth (e.g., responsibility for self-change).

3. Hans is now more aware of the impact of self-change on his own self-identity (intrapersonal) and his social development (interpersonal). He can now take responsibility for his development and change.

True or False

1. True. Labeling a child limits his or her chances for change (e.g., "He is bad at math," results in the self-fulfilling prophecy of the child believing that he is "bad" and performing "poorly.").

2. True. The child couldn't perform the task before, and now he or she has new expertise or maturity (e.g., he or she has changed, and rewarding this mediates self-change).

Define

Self-change is the recognition, acceptance, and monitoring of continual change that occurs within oneself.

Modify

Any statement that encourages the student to try to change or improve (e.g.,"That is a good attempt and with practice you will improve.").

Search for the Optimistic Alternative
(Pages 99–100)

Case Study

1. Nellie does mediate the optimistic alternative by highlighting the positive aspects of Garvan's life and dispelling his negative ideas.

2. Garvan tends to transfer his negative feelings to all aspects of his life. He feels so low that doing drugs seems the only alternative to "lift "his spirits.

3. Your own input. Think of strategies that would direct Garvan on a positive course of action and that would help him see that there are alternatives.

True or False

1. True.

2. False. It is important to highlight and reward positive behaviors also—thus creating more positive options.

Define

Search for the optimistic alternative is a cognitive/affective state of anticipating and working toward positive outcomes.

Modify

Any statement that highlights what the individual can do as opposed to can't do.

Sense of Belonging (Pages 108–109)

Case Study

1. The teacher has put forward the idea of Chang's interconnectedness with people and events of the past.

2. Chang discovers that he belongs to an ancestral line of families who have made history. This may cause him to reflect on his impact on future generations of family.

3. Your own example.

True or False

1. True.

2. False. It is important that the child sees his or her behavior in terms of societal norms (e.g., that they are part of a society/culture).

Define

Sense of belonging is the socio-affective recognition by individuals that they are part of a proximal and global family with whom they share experiences.

Modify

Any statement that emphasizes the importance of a cultural heritage and the interconnectedness of human beings—"It is good to study your culture's customs so that you can understand your parents and yourself better."

PART III. METACOGNITION: COGNITIVE FUNCTIONS AND DYSFUNCTIONS

Input (Pages 136–137)

Identify the Following Input Dysfunctions

1. Impaired understanding of temporal concepts.

2. Impulsive exploration of a learning situation.

3. Impaired data gathering.

4. Impaired understanding of spatial concepts.

5. Impaired understanding of temporal concepts.

6. Impaired receptive verbal tools.

7. Impaired ability to conserve constancy.

8. Impaired capacity to consider more than one source of information.

Match the Cognitive Dysfunctions

1. d
2. h
3. g
4. f
5. c
6. a
7. b
8. e

Elaboration (Pages 170–171)

Identify the Following Elaboration Dysfunctions

1. Episodic grasp of reality.
2. Impaired elaboration of cognitive categories.
3. Lack of need for logical evidence.
4. Inability to engage in spontaneous comparative behavior.
5. Inaccurate definition of the problem.
6. Impaired need for spontaneous summative behavior.
7. Inability to project virtual relationships.
8. Impaired strategies for hypothesis testing.
9. Narrow and limited mental field.
10. Lack of planning behavior.
11. Inability to internalize events.
12. Impaired ability to select relevant cues.
13. Restricted use of inferential-hypothetical thinking.

Match the Cognitive Dysfunctions

1. j
2. e
3. h
4. c
5. f
6. b
7. l
8. d
9. i
10. k
11. a
12. m
13. g

Output (Pages 192–193)

Identify the Following Output Dysfunctions

1. Impaired expressive verbal tools.
2. Trial-and-error output response.
3. Impaired data output.
4. Impaired visual transport.
5. Impulsive, acting-out behavior.
6. Egocentric communication modalities.
7. Blocking output response.

Match the Cognitive Dysfunctions

1. d
2. c
3. e
4. f
5. g
6. b
7. a

PART IV. METATASK: THE COGNITIVE MAP

Word Categories Task (Page 204)

Herbs	*Fruit*	*Vegetable*	*Dairy Product*
basil, parsley, fennel, mint	orange, apple, apricot, grape	carrot, celery, lettuce, potato	yogurt, cream, custard, milk

Analysis According to the Cognitive Map (Pages 204–205)

Task: Word Categories

Content

1. The content is a list of everyday words—simple vocabulary relating to food.

2. The list of words could be varied to include other subject matter besides food. It could be that the student is unfamiliar with some of the words (e.g., fennel or yogurt) and hence the subject matter would impact negatively on the ability to do the task. Learners would have difficulty grouping an item if they did not know what the item was. Changing the list of words to a subject familiar to the learner would aid the task of categorization.

Modality

1. The task is presented in the written modality—as written words.

2. Instead of presenting a list of written words, pictures could be used or diagrams or words presented verbally. Thus the modality could be changed from written words to pictorial or auditory (spoken words).

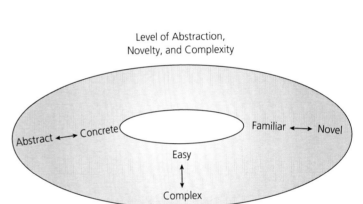

Levels of Abstraction, Novelty, and Complexity

1. The task is presented at a relatively abstract level (written words to be categorized in a table). To make it more concrete, actual objects (the food items) could be presented for the learner to physically put into groups.

2. The learner can work with the teacher or a more competent peer initially while the task of categorization is explained. The teacher can model and talk out loud as they work together and thus scaffold the task and provide practice with a number of different examples so that the task of categorization becomes familiar.

3. Easier grouping tasks can be presented to the learner-groups that are common or only have two groups and a few items to sort into these groups (e.g., sort into colors or sort into fruit and vegetable). The groups could gradually be made more complex in number of categories and number of items.

Cognitive Operation

1. Thinking skills involved in a categorization activity require a number of sequential skills including

- Initial identification of the object or item
- Differentiation of the criteria for including an object or item in a groups
- Comparisons of the object or items according to the criteria for inclusion in a group
- Finally putting items into a group based on the criteria for that group

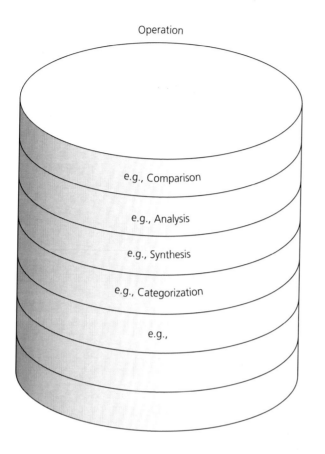

2. Each one of these thinking skills can be taught separately and sequentially to the learner to identify where the cognitive dysfunction occurs.

- Identification involves clear perception and receptive verbal tools at the input phase
- Differentiation involves attention to detail and attention to more than one source of information
- Comparisons and selecting relevant cues and looking at similarities and differences according to the relevant cues
- Grouping involves logical evidence and clear output responses

Resource B

*Mediated Learning
Experience Rating Scale*

This rating scale comprises a list of mediational activities that may occur in a classroom. The activities are grouped into ten sections according to the main criterion of MLE. The rating scale offers the opportunity to rate the quality of mediation being exercised by a mediator, such as a teacher.

RATING

The evaluation should be carried out using the following ratings:

No Opportunity. The lesson did not permit the occurrence of the MLE activity/approach.

Missed Opportunity. The teacher did not implement the MLE activity/approach when the situation allowed for it.

Usually Implemented. The MLE activity was consistently and successfully implemented.

Sometimes Implemented. The MLE activity was occasionally implemented.

Negation. The teacher's activity/approach was insufficient or in opposition to MLE.

The activities/approaches under each criterion are not exhaustive. Any additional or different examples can be listed under the heading "Other."

MEDIATED LEARNING EXPERIENCE

Rating Scale

12 Criteria

Description of MLE Activity	No Opportunity	Missed Opportunity	Usually Implemented	Sometimes Implemented	Negation	Description of Activity That Is Insufficient or In Contradiction to MLE
Intentionality and Reciprocity						
1. Teacher arouses students' interest and motivation						1. Teacher fails to engage students
2. Students ask questions relevant to the subject matter						2. Students do not participate in relevant discussion
3. Teacher gives appropriate feedback to students' verbal contribution						3. Teacher is insensitive to students' verbal contribution
4. Teacher gives appropriate feedback to students' written contribution						4. Teacher fails to meaningfully comment on students' written contribution
5. Teacher is willing to re-explain when work is not understood						5. Teacher is not cognizant of the need for re-explanation
6. Teacher comes prepared and creates a sense of anticipation by changing classroom atmosphere						6. Teacher does not prepare adequately for the lesson and fails to create enthusiasm
7. Other						7. Other

Description of MLE Activity	No Opportunity	Missed Opportunity	Usually Implemented	Sometimes Implemented	Negation	Description of Activity That Is Insufficient or In Contradiction to MLE
Meaning						
1. The teacher explains the importance focusing						1. The teacher fails to provide the purpose or value of a subject or relevance of activities or subjects
2. The teacher explains the reason for focusing on a subject						2. The teacher focuses on a subject without giving explicit reasons
3. The teacher transforms material by changing frequency and/or intensity of presentation						3. The teacher fails to vary presentation, which would convey to students the importance or value of a subject
4. The teacher gives positive or negative feedback to student responses						4. The teacher responds indifferently to student responses
5. The teacher asks "how" and "why" questions—process questions						5. The teacher asks more "who" and "what" questions—content questions
6. Other						6. Other

Description of MLE Activity	No Opportunity	Missed Opportunity	Usually Implemented	Sometimes Implemented	Negation	Description of Activity That Is Insufficient or In Contradiction to MLE
Transcendence						
1. The teacher explains a concept or principle beyond the scope of the present subject matter						1. The teacher fails to bridge concepts to related subject matter
2. The teacher relates the subject of a lesson to previous or future subjects						2. The teacher presents each subject as an isolated and unrelated set of information and ideas
3. The teacher explains how the underlying process to solving a problem can be applied to a variety of situations						3. The teacher fails to show how one problem-solving approach can be applied to a variety of situations
4. The teacher promotes the use of work habits that are useful beyond present needs						4. The teacher fails to show how specific work habits may be used in a different context
5. Other						5. Other

Description of MLE Activity	No Opportunity	Missed Opportunity	Usually Implemented	Sometimes Implemented	Negation	Description of Activity That Is Insufficient or In Contradiction to MLE
Competence						
1. The teacher selects and presents material appropriate to the students' levels of development						1. The teacher fails to take into account the students' levels of development when selecting and presenting material
2. The teacher phrases questions according to the students' levels of competence						2. The teacher's questions are not presented at an appropriate level
3. The teacher encourages students to be aware of their progress relative to their own standards						3. The teacher measures student progress only according to the class average
4. The teacher breaks down a complex task into its simpler parts in order to reduce anxiety						4. The teacher fails to reduce anxiety by showing how a complex task can be simplified
5. The teacher praises successful steps toward completing a task						5. The teacher praises only the successful completion of a task
6. The teacher rewards participation in an activity						6. The teacher does not reward participation in an activity
7. Other						7. Other

Description of MLE Activity	No Opportunity	Missed Opportunity	Usually Implemented	Sometimes Implemented	Negation	Description of Activity That Is Insufficient or In Contradiction to MLE
Self-Regulation and Control of Behavior						
1. The teacher instills in the students behavior conducive to learning—good classroom management						1. The teacher fails to instill in the students behavior conducive to learning—bad classroom management
2. The teacher restrains the inappropriate impulsiveness of students						2. The teacher fails to check inappropriate impulsiveness
3. The teacher encourages self-dicipline						3. The teacher fails to encourage self-discipline
4. The teacher models respect, commitment, and perseverance in classroom activities						4. The teacher fails to demonstrate sustained interest and commitment in classroom activities
5. Other						5. Other

Description of MLE Activity	No Opportunity	Missed Opportunity	Usually Implemented	Sometimes Implemented	Negation	Description of Activity That Is Insufficient or In Contradiction to MLE
Sharing						
1. The teacher applies effective group-teaching methods						1. The teacher fails to apply effective group-teaching methods
2. The teacher encourages students to share their work experiences with each other						2. The teacher discourages students from working cooperatively
3. The teacher shares his or her approach to solving tasks with students						3. The teacher fails to verbalize (talk through) his or her problem-solving strategy
4. The teacher encourages students to help each other and facilitates peer tutoring						4. The teacher always insists on individual work
5. The teacher encourages students to listen to each other						5. The teacher fails to encourage active listening when other students are responding
6. The teacher encourages students to empathize with the feelings of others						6. The teacher fails to promote in the students a tolerance and understanding of another point of view
7. The teacher selects subject matter that emphasizes the importance of cooperation						7. The teacher encourages competition to the detriment of cooperation
8. Other						8. Other

Description of MLE Activity	No Opportunity	Missed Opportunity	Usually Implemented	Sometimes Implemented	Negation	Description of Activity That Is Insufficient or In Contradiction to MLE
Individuation						
1. The teacher accepts divergent approaches to problem solving						1. The teacher communicates that there is only one correct way to solve a problem
2. The teacher encourages independent and original thinking and provides opportunities for innovative work						2. The teacher promotes conformity and discourages individual creativity
3. The teacher lets students choose part of their classroom activities and encourages diversity in the use of free time						3. The teacher is not receptive to student's suggestions and promotes uniformity of activities
4. The teacher enhances positive aspects of multiculturalism						4. The teacher exhibits cultural bias and does not integrate different world views
5. The teacher supports the right of the student to be different						5. The teacher fails to promote acceptance of individual differences
6. The teacher refrains from asking for total identification with his or her values and beliefs						6. The teacher insists on total identification with his or her values and beliefs
7. Other						7. Other

Description of MLE Activity	No Opportunity	Missed Opportunity	Usually Implemented	Sometimes Implemented	Negation	Description of Activity That Is Insufficient or In Contradiction to MLE
Goal Planning						
1. The teacher fosters the students' need and ability to set realistic goals						1. The teacher's inappropriate expectations result in the students setting unrealistic goals
2. The teacher encourages perseverance and patience in the pursuit of goals						2. The teacher allows the students to give up on a task as soon as it becomes difficult
3. The teacher explains to students the strategy underlying goal planning						3. The teacher fails to demonstrate the process of setting and achieving goals
4. The teacher develops in the students the need and ability to review and modify goals according to changing needs and circumstances						4. The teacher fails to develop in the students the need and ability to review and modify goals according to changing needs and circumstances
5. The teacher models goal-directed behavior by setting clear goals for each lesson and for learning in general						5. The teacher has no clear objectives and fails to provide a structure for reaching them
6. The teacher instills an autonomous attitude in students about their future						6. The teacher is prescriptive and makes decisions for the students' futures
7. Other						7. Other

Description of MLE Activity	No Opportunity	Missed Opportunity	Usually Implemented	Sometimes Implemented	Negation	Description of Activity That Is Insufficient or In Contradiction to MLE
Challenge						
1. The teacher encourages intellectual curiosity						1. The teacher does not encourage intellectual curiosity
2. The teacher encourages originality and creativity						2. The teacher instills conformist behavior and discourages divergent thinking
3. The teacher makes available to the students challenging, novel, and complex situations						3. The teacher adheres to the 'tried-and-tested' approach and presents conventional tasks to students
4. The teacher encourages students to create their own examples and to present them to the class						4. The teacher inhibits original approaches when engaging in an activity
5. The teacher helps the students anticipate the satisfaction of completing a task						5. The teacher fails to promote intrinsic motivation to complete a complex task
6. The teacher encourages students to persevere with difficult tasks						6. The teacher fails to instill perseverance with difficult tasks
7. Other						7. Other

Description of MLE Activity	No Opportunity	Missed Opportunity	Usually Implemented	Sometimes Implemented	Negation	Description of Activity That Is Insufficient or In Contradiction to MLE
Self-Change						
1. The teacher promotes self-evaluation of individual progress						1. The teacher fails to develop an awareness of self-evaluation and individual progress
2. The teacher encourages students to use internal criteria for measuring progress						2. The teacher explicity evaluates students relative to class standards and encourages comparison of grades
3. The teacher deemphasizes labeling of students						3. The teacher's consistent use of labeling results in the students acting out these expectations
4. The teacher generates an awareness of change within oneself, and in relationships with others and the environment						4. The teacher fails to create an awareness of change within oneself and in relationships with others and the envionment
5. The teacher models self-change by sharing his or her growth and learning experiences						5. The teacher fails to modify his or her attitudes or approaches to new situations
6. Other						6. Other

Description of MLE Activity	No Opportunity	Missed Opportunity	Usually Implemented	Sometimes Implemented	Negation	Description of Activity That Is Insufficient or In Contradiction to MLE
Optimistic Alternative						
1. Teacher emphasizes the positive aspects of a learning task						1. Teacher emphasizes only the negative side of the task
2. Teacher encourages students to perceive the benefits of completing a task						2. Teacher fails to acknowledge the benefits of completing a task
3. Teacher engages students in an active exploration to find the best alternatives in solving a problem						3. Teacher engages students in problem solving that look for faults
4. Teacher focuses student on all that they can achieve						4. Teacher focuses on the students faults and weaknesses
5. Teacher de-emphasizes labels, e.g., ADHD, to avoid limiting potential						5. Teacher applies labels that limit the potentials of students
6. Other						6. Other

Description of MLE Activity	No Opportunity	Missed Opportunity	Usually Implemented	Sometimes Implemented	Negation	Description of Activity That Is Insufficient or In Contradiction to MLE
Sense of Belonging						
1. Teacher fosters students' needs to reflect on their origins						1. Teacher ignores any link of the students to their origins
2. Teacher sets tasks that encourage students to review their cultural affiliations						2. Teacher avoids tasks that cause the student to examine their cultural affiliations
3. Teacher engages students in an active search to build a family tree						3. Teacher ignores activities that address other family members
4. Teacher reminds students of their interconnectedness with, and influence on, the society in which they live						4. Teacher fails to acknowledge student's connections and influences on society as a whole
5. Teacher encourages students to research, celebrate, and preserve their culture for future generations						5. Teacher is not cognizant of the cultural diversity in the class and fails to structure activities to perpetuate these cultures
6. Other						6. Other

Resource C

Glossary

abstract   ideas or concepts that are not concrete

affective   pertaining to emotions and feelings

autonomy   self-sufficiency and independence of the individual

bridging   transferring learned strategies and principles to other domains

closure   completion

cognitive   pertaining to thinking skills or mental processes

concepts   ideas; general notions

cooperative   learning working together for mutual benefit

culture   According to Feuerstein, culture does not refer to a closed or static list of behaviors, but to a process by which knowledge, values, and beliefs are transmitted across generations.

decentrate   the ability to see things from different perspectives

disequilibrium   a state of imbalance; a problem

dysfunction   impaired or abnormal function

dysfunctional   impaired or disabled

empathy   understanding and identifying with another's feelings; putting oneself in another's shoes

empower   to develop an ability to act autonomously

episodic   grasp of reality the perception of reality as consisting of separate, isolated, and unrelated entities

external   locus of control attributing success or failure to outside forces; not taking responsibility for one's successes or failures

function   a specific task

hypothesis   a supposition made as a basis for reasoning

impulsivity   rushing into a task and acting without thought of the consequences

infer	to deduce or conclude from a variety of examples
interaction	the interconnection, interdependence, and movement among objects, events, ideas, or people
interiorization	solving a problem in one's head
internal	locus of control taking responsibility for one's own success or failure
intrinsic	the basic nature of a person or thing
intrinsic motivation	a desire to complete a task for its own value rather than for external rewards
instrumental enrichment	Feuerstein's program to enhance cognition and re-mediate dysfunction
lateral thinking	problem solving in which the individual attempts to view the problem from many angles rather than to search for a direct, straightforward solution
logical evidence	reasons available as proof to substantiate facts
manipulate	to skillfully arrange (objects, facts, subjects, or emotions)
mediator	According to Feuerstein, a mediator is an experienced, intentioned, and active human being, prototypically the parent and later the teacher, who interacts with the child and interprets and explains both present and historic reality to him or her. The quality of this interaction will influence the degree of later learning or cognitive modifiability of which the individual will be capable.
mediatee	the person who receives and interacts with the mediator
mental act	a stage of thinking
mental field	the area of operating in one's mind
mental image	a picture in one's mind
metacognition	thinking about thinking; an awareness and understanding of one's thought processes and behavior
metalearning	learning that goes beyond the basic fundaments
metatask	a task designed to enhance metacognition
metathinking	higher levels of processing thought
modality	the mode or manner in which something is expressed or communicated (e.g., MLE can be expressed in a number of modalities such as language, gesture, observation)
modeling	demonstrating a type of behavior or action in order to illustrate something
modifiability	ability to alter and modify

multiculturalism	the diversity of cultures
needs system	the internalized environmental demands that are made on an individual
operationalize	to show the application or use of
peer tutoring	learning from fellow students
revisualize	to make visible in one's mind a distinct mental image
rote recall	the regurgitation of facts without necessarily understanding them
self-disclosure	expressing one's feelings and opinions
self-monitor	assessing and regulating one's behavior
stimuli	any objects, events, or ideas in the environment
structural	involves organization and integration of the components that make up our thinking
summation	finding the total; giving a résumé
transcend	to rise above, surpass, span, go beyond
virtual relationship	the essence of a relationship, rather than the actuality
visual transport	moving a mental image in one's mind

References

Bandura, A. (1986). *Social foundations of thought and action: A social cognitive theory.* Englewood Cliffs, NJ: Prentice Hall.

Bronfenbrenner, U. (1979). *The ecology of human development: Experiments by nature and design.* Cambridge, MA: Harvard University Press.

Feuerstein, R. (1980). *Instrumental Enrichment.* Baltimore, MD: University Park Press.

Feuerstein, R. (1979). *The dynamic assessment of retarded performers.* Baltimore, MD: University Park Press.

Feuerstein, R., & Jensen, M. (1980). Instrumental Enrichment: Theoretical basis, goals and instruments. *Educational Forum, 44*(4), 401–23.

Feuerstein, R., et al. (1986). *L.P.A.D.: Learning potential assessment device manual.* Jerusalem: Hadassah-Wizo-Canada Research Institute.

Feuerstein, R., et al. (1982). Learning to learn: MLE and IE. *Special Services in the Schools, 3*(1–2), 49–82.

Feuerstein, R., Rand, Y., & Hoffman, M. (1979). *The dynamic assessment of retarded performers: The learning potential assessment device, theory instruments and techniques.* Baltimore, MD: University Park Press.

Feuerstein, R., Rand, Y., Hoffman, M., & Miller, R. (1980). *Instrumental Enrichment: An intervention program for cognitive modifiability.* Baltimore, MD: University Park Press.

Feuerstein, R., Rand, Y., & Rynders, J. (1988). *Don't accept me as I am: Helping "retarded" people to excel.* New York: Plenum Press.

Flavell, J. H. (1979). Metacognition and cognitive monitoring: A new area of cognitive-developmental inquiry. *American Psychologist, 34,* 906–911.

Frankl. V. E. (1985). *Man's search for meaning.* New York: Washington Square Press.

Gilg, J. E. (1990). The use of mediated learning to enhance the educational effectiveness of school programs for high-risk youth. *International Journal of Cognitive Education and Mediated Learning, 1*(1), 63–71.

Gould, S. J. (1981). *The mismeasure of man.* Harmondsworth, UK: Pelican Books.

Greenberg, K. H. (1990). *Cognet: Parent's manual.* University of Tennessee. (unpublished)

Greenberg, K. H. (1990). Mediated learning in the classroom. *International Journal of Cognitive Education and Mediated Learning, 1*(81), 33–44.

Greenberg, K. H., & Kaniel, S. A. (1990). Thousand year transition for Ethiopian immigrants to Israel: The effects of modifiability, mediated learning and cultural transmission. *International Journal of Cognitive Education and Mediated Learning, 1*(2), 137–142.

Hayes, S. C., et al. (1985). Self-reinforcement effects: An artifact of social standard setting? *Journal of Applied Behaviour Analysis, 18,* 201–214.

Hopson, B., & Scally, M. (1981). *Life skills teaching.* London: McGraw-Hill.

Iveson, C. (2002). Solution Focused Brief Therapy. *Advances in Psychiatric Treatment, 8,* 149–156.

Johnson, D. W., & Johnson, R. (1974). Instructional goal structure: Cooperative, competitive, or individualistic. *Review of Educational Research, 44,* 213–240.

Kipling, R. (1902). *Just so stories.* Doubleday & Company, Inc..

Kozulin, A. (1990). Mediation: Psychological activity and psychological tools. *International Journal of Cognitive Education and Mediated Learning, 1*(2), 151–159.

Mentis, M., Dunn, M. et al. (1996). *Mediated learning in and out of the classroom.* Glenview, IL: IRI/SkyLight Training and Publishing Inc.

Morgan, M. (1985). Self-monitoring of attained subgoals in private study. *Journal of Educational Psychology, 77,* 623–630.

Rosenthal, R., & Jacobson, L. (1968). *Pygmalion in the classroom.* New York: Rinehart and Winston.

Savell, J. M., et al. (1986). Empirical status of Feuerstein's "Instrumental Enrichment" (FIE) techniques as a method of teaching thinking skills. *Review of Educational Research, 56*(4), 383–409.

Sharron, H. (1987). *Changing children's minds: Feuerstein's revolution in the teaching of intelligence.* London: Souvenir Press.

Skuy, M., et al. (1990). Combining Instrumental Enrichment and creativity/socioemotional development for disadvantaged gifted adolescents in Soweto. Pt. 1. *International Journal of Cognitive Education and Mediated Learning, 1*(1), 25–31.

Skuy, M., et al. (1990). Combining Instrumental Enrichment and creativity/socioemotional development for disadvantaged gifted adolescents in Soweto. Pt. 2. *International Journal of Cognitive Education and Mediated Learning, 1*(2), 93–102.

Skuy, M., & Mentis, M. (1992). Applications and adaptations of Feuerstein's Instrumental Enrichment programme among the disadvantaged population in South Africa. In J. Carlson (Ed.), *Cognition and educational practice: An international perspective, Volume I (Part B)* (pp. 105–127). Greenwich, CT: JAI Press.

Skuy, M., & Mentis, M. (1990). Application of instrumental enrichment programme in South Africa. Proceedings of the HSRC Conference on Cognitive Development, 1 November, in Pretoria, South Africa.

Slavin, R. E. (1987). Ability grouping and student achievement in elementary schools: A best-evidence synthesis. *Review of Educational Research, 57,* 293–336.

Sternberg, R. J. (1988). *The triarchic mind: A new theory of human intelligence.* New York: Viking.

Tomlinson, C. A. (2001). *How to differentiate instruction in mixed ability classroom* (2nd ed.). Alexandria, VA: ASCD Publication.

Tzuriel, D., & Eran, Z. (1990a). Inferential cognitive modifiability of kibbutz young children as a function of mother-child Mediated Learning Experience (MLE) interactions. *International Journal of Cognitive Education and Mediated Learning, 1*(2), 103–117.

Tzuriel, D., & Eran, Z. (1990b). Mediated Learning Experience and cognitive modifiability: Testing the effects of distal and proximal factors by structural equation model. *International Journal of Cognitive Education and Mediated Learning, 1*(2), 119–135.

Vygotsky, L. S. (1987). Thinking and speech (N. Minick, Trans.). In R. W. Rieber & A. S. Carton (Eds.), *The collected works of L. S. Vygotsky: Vol. 1. Problems of general psychology* (pp. 39–285). New York: Plenum. (Original work published 1934)

Wallace, B. & Adams, H. (Eds.) (1993). *Worldwide perspectives on the gifted disadvantaged.* Bicester, Oxford, UK: AB Academic Publishers.

Index

**CORWIN
PRESS**

The Corwin Press logo—a raven striding across an open book—represents the union of courage and learning. Corwin Press is committed to improving education for all learners by publishing books and other professional development resources for those serving the field of PreK–12 education. By providing practical, hands-on materials, Corwin Press continues to carry out the promise of its motto: **"Helping Educators Do Their Work Better."**